Maths
for Key Stage 2

It's a Maths extravaganza from CGP!

This brilliant CGP book is bursting with Maths questions for 7-8 year olds.
They're split into three difficulty levels to suit pupils of all abilities
— with plenty of fun challenge pages added in for variety.

Every topic from the Year 3 Programme of Study is covered,
and it's all perfectly matched to the latest National Curriculum!

What CGP is all about

Our sole aim here at CGP is to produce the highest quality books —
carefully written, immaculately presented and
jam-packed with helpful content.

Then we work our socks off to get them out to you
— at the cheapest possible prices.

Year 3

Contents

Section 3 — Multiplication and Division

Section 4 — Fractions

Section 5 — Measurement

Section 6 — Geometry

Section 7 — Statistics

Published by CGP

ISBN: 978 1 78294 796 7

Editors: Tom Carney, Joanna Daniels, Liam Dyer, Zoe Fenwick, Shaun Harrogate, Hannah Roscoe, Ruth Wilbourne, Dawn Wright

With thanks to Glenn Rogers, Clare Selway and Ben Train for the proofreading.
With thanks to Ana Pungartnik for the copyright research.

Printed by Elanders Ltd, Newcastle upon Tyne.
Clipart from Corel®
Cover image: © iStock.com/FrankRamspott

About This Book

This book covers every topic that you need to learn in Year 3 Maths.
We've packed it full of questions and made sure there is the right practice for everyone.

You'll find examples at the start of each topic.
These are great reminders of how you might
answer some of the questions on the topic.

Topics are each split into three Sets:

* **Set A** is perfect for getting to grips with the Year 3 topics.

* **Set B** is ideal practice if you're up to
  speed with the Year 3 topics.

* **Set C** offers an extra stretch if you're
  comfortable with the Year 3 topics.

Your teacher will let you know which Set you should work on.

At the end of each topic, the objective sums up the
maths skills you've learnt. You can use the tick boxes
to show how confident you feel about the topic.

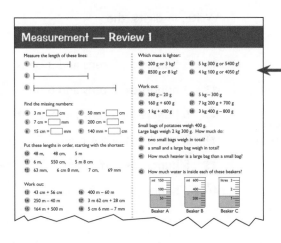

After every few topics there's a **Review** page
with even more practice questions — a perfect way
to recap all of the topics you've learnt leading up to it.

Each Section ends with some **Challenges**. These are a fun
and interesting way to practise lots of the skills and topics
you've covered in the Section.

They include loads of different questions and activities — you
might have to draw, make shapes, work with other classmates,
or create your own games!

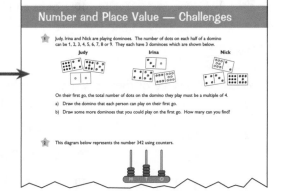

The <u>Answer Book</u> for this Year 3 Textbook has answers to all the questions. It also includes a mapping of
the <u>Programme of Study</u>, and a suggested <u>Scheme of Work</u> that teachers can follow throughout the year.

Free printable resources including blank clock faces, scales and number lines can be found on our website:

www.cgpbooks.co.uk/KS2MathsResources

Place Value

The value of a digit changes depending on its place in a number.
Three-digit numbers are made up of hundreds, tens and ones.

£786

Examples

In 325, which place is the 5 in?

Hundreds	Tens	Ones
3	2	5

The 5 is in the **ones** place.

What is the value of the 7 in 786?

Hundreds	Tens	Ones
7	8	6

7 hundreds or **700**

Set A

Write down the place (hundreds, tens or ones) of each of these digits:

1. 1 in 261
2. 4 in 453
3. 6 in 768
4. 3 in 139
5. 8 in 528
6. 4 in 477

Look at the number 534.

7. Which digit is in the ones place?
8. Which digit is in the tens place?

Look at the number 629.

9. Which digit is in the tens place?
10. Which digit is in the hundreds place?
11. What is the value of the 9?

What is the value of the:

12. 2 in 129?
13. 7 in 754?
14. 3 in 463?
15. 8 in 891?
16. 2 in 442?
17. 5 in 656?
18. 9 in 907?

Set B

What is the value of each underlined digit?

1. 2<u>6</u>8
2. <u>5</u>41
3. 83<u>3</u>
4. <u>9</u>72
5. 16<u>4</u>
6. 3<u>5</u>9

Look at the number 743. Find the missing word:

7. The 4 is in the ☐ place.
8. The 7 is in the ☐ place.

Look at the number 456. Write the new number you make if you swap the:

9. tens and ones digits.
10. ones and hundreds digits.

Write, in digits, the following numbers:

11. 3 hundreds, 8 tens and 3 ones
12. 4 hundreds, 2 tens and 6 ones
13. 6 hundreds, 3 tens and 9 ones
14. 2 hundreds and 4 ones
15. 5 hundreds and 7 tens
16. 7 hundreds and 9 tens

Set C

What is the value of the:

1. 5 in 485?
2. 9 in 192?
3. 7 in 731?
4. 8 in 820?
5. 4 in 547?
6. 3 in 613?
7. 2 in 924?

Write, in digits, the numbers being described below:

8. 6 hundreds, 9 ones
9. 8 tens, 9 hundreds
10. 2 tens, 4 hundreds, 7 ones
11. 3 ones, 5 tens and 1 hundred
12. 1 one, 5 hundreds and 5 tens
13. 4 tens, 3 ones and 9 hundreds

Use all three of these digit cards to answer the questions below:

| 7 | 2 | 8 |

Write two numbers you can make with:

14. an 8 in the hundreds position.
15. a 7 in the hundreds position.
16. a 2 in the tens position.

I know the place value of the digits in a three-digit number.

Writing Numbers — 1

You should already be able to write numbers up to 100 using digits.
In Year 3, you need to be able to do this for numbers up to 1000.

Examples

Write two hundred
and thirty using digits.

200 + 30 = **230**

Write five hundred
and seven using digits.

500 + 7 = **507**

An shop sells eight hundred and forty-three vases.
Write this number using digits.

800 + 40 + 3 = **843**

Set A

Find the missing digits:

1. ☐4 = eighty-four
2. ☐00 = two hundred
3. 50☐ = five hundred
4. 40☐ = four hundred and one
5. 3☐2 = three hundred and twelve
6. 7☐☐ = seven hundred and forty-six

Write these as numbers:

7. 4 hundred and 30
8. 6 hundred and 19
9. 3 hundred and 12
10. 7 hundred and 45
11. 2 hundred and 8
12. 5 hundred and 7
13. 8 hundred and 3

Write these amounts using digits:

14. Four hundred and thirteen
15. Five hundred and sixty
16. Six hundred and twenty-two
17. Seven hundred and twenty-seven
18. Nine hundred and thirty-five
19. One thousand

Set B

Are the following true or false?

1. 477 = Four hundred and seventy-seven
2. 639 = Six hundred and twenty-nine
3. 875 = Eight hundred and fifty-seven
4. 222 = Two hundred and twenty-two

Write these amounts using digits:

5. Three hundred
6. Four hundred and nine
7. Five hundred and twenty
8. Two hundred and fourteen
9. Six hundred and ninety-eight
10. Nine hundred and forty-two
11. One thousand

Write in digits:

12. Seven hundred and ninety-two
13. Eight hundred and thirty-seven
14. A factory makes nine hundred and forty-seven teapots in a day. Write this amount using digits.

Set C

Write these amounts using digits:

1. Five hundred and nineteen
2. Six hundred and sixteen
3. Six hundred and four
4. Seven hundred and forty-one
5. Eight hundred and thirty
6. Nine hundred and thirteen
7. One thousand

These labels show the number of sweets in some jars.
Rewrite the labels using digits:

8. Five hundred and ten
9. Seven hundred and forty-seven
10. Four hundred and eight
11. Nine hundred and fifty-six

Find the missing digits:

12. Eight hundred and sixty-three = ☐6☐
13. Nine hundred and thirty-two = 9☐☐
14. Two thousand and seventeen = 2☐☐☐
15. Three thousand, one hundred and nine = 3☐☐☐

I can write numbers up to 1000 using digits.

Writing Numbers — 2

As well as writing numbers using digits, you also need to know how to write numbers using words.

Examples

Write 319 in words.

Three hundred and nineteen

Write 705 in words.

Seven hundred and five

An ice cream van sells 846 ice lollies. Write this number using words.

Eight hundred and forty-six

Set A

Write in words:

1. 93
2. 100
3. 200
4. 360
5. 418
6. 512
7. 617

Find the missing word:

8. 250 = two hundred and ▢
9. 475 = four hundred and ▢-five
10. 632 = ▢ hundred and thirty-two
11. 943 = ▢ hundred and forty-three
12. 517 = five hundred and ▢

Write these numbers using words:

13. 561
14. 633
15. 162
16. 345
17. 564
18. 852
19. 1000

Set B

Write in words:

1. 400
2. 580
3. 730
4. 106
5. 217
6. 903
7. 849

Find the missing word:

8. 480 = four hundred and ▢
9. 502 = ▢ hundred and two
10. 313 = ▢ hundred and thirteen
11. 762 = seven hundred and ▢-two
12. 975 = ▢ hundred and seventy-five

A chef records how many plates of food he makes in one month. Write his results using words:

13. 529 plates of lasagne
14. 803 bowls of soup
15. 641 portions of apple pie
16. 992 plates of roast beef
17. 738 bowls of chicken stew

Set C

Write in words:

1. 702
2. 817
3. 593
4. 622
5. 483
6. 954
7. 1000

This table shows how many people visited a castle in four months:

May	June	July	August
936	727	914	865

Write in words:

8. the number of visitors in May.
9. the number of visitors in July.
10. the number of visitors in August.

Write the even numbers in words:

11. 681, 792, 593
12. 424, 537, 389
13. 976, 855, 841

Write the odd numbers in words:

14. 733, 950, 854
15. 632, 579, 780
16. 1000, 946, 973

I can write numbers up to 1000 using words.

Partitioning

Partitioning a number means splitting it up into different parts.
You can split numbers in different ways — take a look at the examples below.

Examples

Partition 463 into hundreds, tens and ones.

463 = 400 + 60 + 3

Partition 825 cm into hundreds and a two-digit number.

825 cm = 800 cm + 25 cm

Set A

Complete each partitioning with the correct number:

1. 102 = 100 + ☐
2. 260 = ☐ + 60
3. 327 = ☐ + 20 + 7
4. 471 = 400 + ☐ + 1
5. 589 = 500 + 80 + ☐
6. 636 = ☐ + 30 + 6

Find the missing numbers to partition these numbers into hundreds, tens and ones:

7. 346 = ☐ + ☐ + 6
8. 519 = ☐ + 10 + ☐
9. 764 = 700 + ☐ + ☐
10. 853 = ☐ + ☐ + 3
11. 991 = ☐ + 90 + ☐

Partition these numbers into hundreds, tens and ones:

12. 119
13. 282
14. 397
15. 564
16. 723
17. 478

Set B

Find the missing numbers to partition these numbers into hundreds, tens and ones:

1. 387 = 300 + ☐ + ☐
2. 594 = ☐ + 90 + ☐
3. 633 = ☐ + ☐ + 3
4. 841 = 800 + ☐ + ☐
5. 925 = ☐ + 20 + ☐

Partition these numbers into hundreds, tens and ones:

6. 279
7. 852
8. 366
9. 417
10. 928
11. 541

Write these partitioned numbers as one number:

12. 700 + 30 + 5
13. 900 + 20 + 4

Partition these numbers into hundreds and a two-digit number:

14. 345
15. 896

Set C

Partition these numbers into hundreds, tens and ones:

1. 907
2. 534
3. 688
4. 210
5. 434
6. 385

Complete each partitioning with the correct numbers:

7. 312 = 300 + ☐
8. 493 = ☐ + 93
9. 554 = 550 + ☐
10. 786 = ☐ + 6
11. 827 = ☐ + 820
12. 915 = 15 + ☐

Write as one number:

13. 900 + 47
14. 780 + 7

Find the missing numbers to partition these into thousands, hundreds, tens and ones:

15. 1023 = 1000 + ☐ + ☐
16. 2490 = 2000 + ☐ + ☐

I can partition three-digit numbers.

Ordering Numbers

Putting numbers in order is a doddle once you get the hang of it.
Just make sure you're always comparing digits with the same place value.

Example

Which of these numbers is the smallest?

(693)   741   753   (626)   759   Look at the hundreds digits: 6 is the smallest.

693   626   Look at the tens digits of 693 and 626: 2 is the smallest, so **626** is the smallest number.

Set A

Which is smaller:

1. 53 or 79?
2. 182 or 341?
3. 267 or 132?
4. 104 or 108?
5. 210 or 201?
6. 386 or 368?
7. 547 or 574?

Complete each sentence with the word 'bigger' or 'smaller':

8. 658 is [ ] than 586.
9. 451 is [ ] than 541.
10. 271 is [ ] than 217.
11. 439 is [ ] than 493.
12. 327 is [ ] than 372.
13. 986 is [ ] than 968.

Put these numbers in order, starting with the smallest:

14. 384   179   216
15. 592   671   498

Put these numbers in order, starting with the largest:

16. 454   531   586
17. 765   727   772

Set B

Which symbol (< or >) should go in each box?

1. 293 [ ] 451
2. 872 [ ] 834
3. 511 [ ] 598
4. 629 [ ] 619
5. 354 [ ] 345
6. 923 [ ] 932

Put these numbers in order, starting with the smallest:

7. 347   581   496   572
8. 725   739   613   648

Put these numbers in order, starting with the largest:

9. 929   637   813   954
10. 759   886   734   821

The box below shows how many grapefruit are in 6 different crates:

514   326   698
558   761   349

Joe stacks the crates in order, starting with the crate with the most grapefruit. How many grapefruit are in:

11. the fourth crate in the stack?
12. the crate at the top of the stack?

Set C

Find the second largest number in each list:

1. 762, 737, 745
2. 238, 269, 252
3. 424, 441, 414
4. 593, 567, 541
5. 822, 834, 856
6. 371, 377, 369

Put these numbers in order, starting with the largest:

7. 844   854   855   845
8. 931   911   913   933
9. Which of the following numbers is greater than 745, but less than 756?

743   765   758   754

A bike shop has 8 bikes for sale. The box below shows the price of each bike:

£616   £738   £549   £620
£581   £694   £663   £650

10. How much is the second cheapest bike?
11. How much is the third most expensive bike?

I can compare and order numbers up to 1000.

Number and Place Value — Review 1

Write down the place of the:

1. 4 in 234
2. 7 in 679
3. 5 in 358
4. 8 in 810
5. 3 in 553
6. 6 in 641
7. 7 in 887
8. 2 in 925

What is the value of:

9. the 3 in 135?
10. the 9 in 429?
11. the 8 in 863?
12. the 2 in 270?
13. the 5 in 959?
14. the 1 in 991?
15. each 6 in 866?
16. each 4 in 454?

Find the missing digits:

17. 1☐3 = one hundred and sixty-three
18. ☐29 = two hundred and twenty-nine
19. 46☐ = four hundred and sixty-five
20. 7☐8 = seven hundred and eighteen
21. ☐☐1 = nine hundred and fifty-one
22. 2☐☐☐ = two thousand, six hundred and fifty-seven

Write these amounts as numbers:

23. 1 hundred and 36
24. 3 hundred and 50
25. 4 hundred and 81
26. 6 hundred and 27
27. 5 hundred and 4
28. 8 hundred and 9

Write each of these numbers using digits:

29. One hundred and thirty
30. Four hundred and sixty-one
31. Five hundred and forty-four
32. Six hundred and thirty-five
33. Eight hundred and seven
34. Nine hundred and ninety-three

Find the missing words:

35. 320 = three hundred and ☐
36. 540 = ☐ hundred and forty
37. 787 = seven hundred and ☐-seven
38. 816 = eight hundred and ☐
39. 953 = ☐ hundred and ☐-three

Write each of these numbers using words:

40. 101
41. 202
42. 316
43. 490
44. 661
45. 784
46. 935
47. 998

Partition these numbers into hundreds, tens and ones:

48. 108
49. 230
50. 369
51. 457
52. 683
53. 725
54. 842
55. 961

Complete each partitioning:

56. 107 = 100 + ☐
57. 242 = 200 + ☐ + 2
58. 436 = ☐ + 30 + ☐
59. 587 = 500 + ☐ + ☐
60. 944 = ☐ + 44
61. 829 = 820 + ☐

Which number is the smallest:

62. 211 or 324?
63. 798 or 789?
64. 641 or 614?
65. 734, 743 or 733?
66. 821, 818 or 812?
67. 966, 969 or 996?

Put these numbers in order, starting with the largest:

68. 398, 425, 297
69. 739, 612, 557
70. 821, 957, 946, 873
71. 431, 484, 476, 495
72. 783, 746, 795, 761
73. 344, 434, 443, 343

Phew! Well done for conquering this mountain of questions.

Number Lines

You can use number lines to show the position and order of numbers.
Make sure you check the scale carefully — it might not go up or down in simple steps.

Example

Which number is the arrow pointing to?

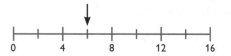

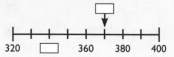

Look at the scale — it's going up in 4s.

Now look at the arrow — it's pointing to a number halfway between 4 and 8. This means the answer is **6**.

Set A

Which number is each arrow pointing to?

1
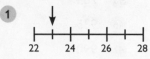

2
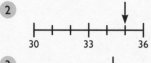

3
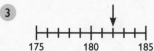

4 What temperature is the thermometer below showing?

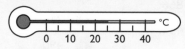

Copy out the scale on the thermometer. Draw and label an arrow pointing to:

5 5 °C

6 35 °C

7 Find the missing values on this number line.

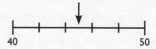

8 Estimate the number that the arrow is pointing to:

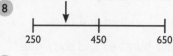

Set B

Which number is each arrow pointing to?

1
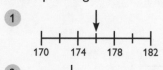

2
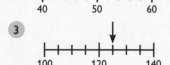

3
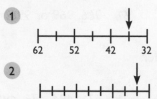

Copy the number line below.

Draw and label an arrow pointing to:

4 614

5 632

6 six hundred and six

7 six hundred and twenty-eight

Estimate the number that each arrow is pointing to:

8
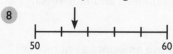

9
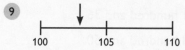

10
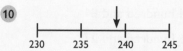

Set C

Which number is each arrow pointing to?

1
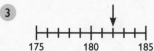

2

3
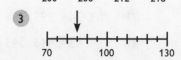

Copy the number line below.

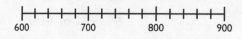

Draw and label an arrow pointing to:

4 six hundred and eighty

5 eight hundred and forty

6 six hundred and twenty

7 seven hundred and sixty

Estimate the number that each arrow is pointing to:

8

9

10
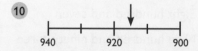

I can read, draw and estimate amounts on number lines.

Counting in Multiples of 4

You can use number lines to count up in 4s. Check out these examples.

Examples

Starting at 0, count forward 4 steps of 4:

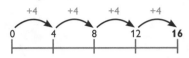

A kangaroo travels 4 m in 1 hop.
How far does it travel in 6 hops?

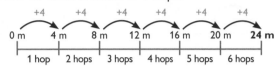

Set A

Starting at 0, count forward:

1. 1 step of 4.
2. 4 steps of 4.
3. 5 steps of 4.

Starting at 4, count forward:

4. 6 steps of 4.
5. 5 steps of 4.
6. 8 steps of 4.

Starting at 40, count back:

7. 2 steps of 4.
8. 3 steps of 4.
9. 5 steps of 4.

Complete these sentences
with the correct number:

10. 16 is ☐ steps of 4 from 4.
11. 28 is ☐ steps of 4 from 4.

How many steps of 4 are there:

12. between 0 and 24?
13. between 4 and 12?
14. between 16 and 28?
15. between 24 and 40?

16. Tamal says, "There are 9 steps of 4 between 16 and 44." Is he correct?

Set B

Starting at 8, count forward:

1. 3 steps of 4.
2. 4 steps of 4.
3. 9 steps of 4.

Starting at 16, count forward:

4. 1 step of 4.
5. 2 steps of 4.
6. 6 steps of 4.

Complete these sentences
with the correct number:

7. 28 is ☐ steps of 4 from 0.
8. 20 is ☐ steps of 4 from 8.
9. 32 is ☐ steps of 4 from 12.

10. Sarah thinks there are 5 steps of 4 between 16 and 40. Keith thinks there are 6 steps. Who is correct?

Reggie starts off with 24 stamps and collects 4 more every week. How many stamps does he have:

11. after 3 weeks?
12. after 6 weeks?

Fran buys 32 cherry scones. Scones come in packs of 4. How many will she have if:

13. she buys 2 more packs?
14. she eats 4 packs?

Set C

Starting at 32, count:

1. forward 2 steps of 4.
2. forward 5 steps of 4.
3. back 7 steps of 4.

Starting at 40, count:

4. forward 4 steps of 4.
5. back 3 steps of 4.
6. back 5 steps of 4.

Find the missing number
in each of these sequences:

7. 12 ☐ 20 24
8. 52 56 60 ☐
9. ☐ 80 ☐ 88

How many steps of 4 are there:

10. between 28 and 44?
11. between 40 and 52?

Galia has 44 carrots. Her horse eats 4 carrots each day. How many carrots are left after:

12. 3 days?
13. 7 days?

14. Frank bakes 84 muffins. He sells them in boxes of 4. How many muffins does he have left if he sells 5 boxes?

I can count in multiples of 4.

Counting in Multiples of 8

Now it's time to start counting in multiples of 8 — you can always use a number line to help you.

Examples

Starting at 8, count forward 3 steps of 8:

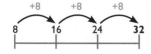

How many steps of 8 are there between 16 and 48?

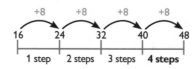

So there are **4 steps** of 8 between 16 and 48.

Set A

Use the number line to help you answer the questions below.

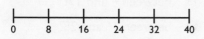

Starting at 0, count forward:

1. 1 step of 8.
2. 3 steps of 8.
3. 5 steps of 8.

Starting at 8, count forward:

4. 3 steps of 8.
5. 6 steps of 8.
6. 7 steps of 8.

How many steps of 8 are there:

7. between 24 and 40?
8. between 72 and 80?

Count in 8s to find the missing number in each of these sequences:

9. 0   8   ☐   24
10. 8   16   24   ☐
11. 32   ☐   48   56
12. 48   ☐   64   72
13. ☐   88   96   104

Set B

Find the missing number in each of these sequences:

1. 16   ☐   32   40
2. 48   56   ☐   72

Starting at 24, count forward:

3. 1 step of 8.
4. 3 steps of 8.
5. 5 steps of 8.

Are the following true or false?

6. 40 is 5 steps of 8 from 0.
7. 48 is 7 steps of 8 from 4.
8. 56 is 5 steps of 8 from 16.

Starting at 72, count:

9. forward 2 steps of 8.
10. back 3 steps of 8.
11. back 6 steps of 8.

12. Chesney has 24 crayons. He gets 4 boxes of 8 crayons for his birthday. How many crayons does he have now?

Mischa has 32 golf balls. They come in packs of 8. How many golf balls will she have if she:

13. buys 4 more packs?
14. gives 3 packs to her brother?

Set C

1. Start at 24 and write down the next 5 multiples of 8.
2. Start at 64 and write down the previous 3 multiples of 8.

Complete these sentences with the correct number:

3. 56 is ☐ steps of 8 from 8.
4. 72 is ☐ steps of 8 from 32.

How many steps of 8 are there are between:

5. 0 and 80?
6. 16 and 40?
7. 32 and 48?
8. 72 and 56?
9. 80 and 24?
10. 72 and 112?

11. Spiders have 8 legs each. Colette's pet spiders have 56 legs in total. She gets 3 more spiders. How many legs do her spiders have in total now?

12. Crumpets are sold in packs of 8. A supermarket has 96 crumpets. Angela buys 1 pack and Eli buys 2 packs. How many crumpets are left in the supermarket?

I can count in multiples of 8.

Counting in Multiples of 50

You already know how to count in multiples of 5 — counting in multiples of 50 is the same, just with an extra 0.

Examples

Starting at 0, count forward 4 steps of 50:

```
   +50    +50    +50    +50
 ⌢      ⌢      ⌢      ⌢
0     50    100   150   200
```

A zoo has 3 giant tortoises. Each tortoise is 50 years old. What is the sum of their ages?

```
      +50        +50        +50
   ⌢          ⌢          ⌢
0      50 years   100 years   150 years

   1 tortoise  2 tortoises  3 tortoises
```

Set A

Count in steps of 50 to find the missing number in each of these sequences:

1. 0 ☐ 100 150
2. 200 250 ☐ 350
3. ☐ 450 500 550
4. 600 ☐ 700 750
5. 800 850 900 ☐

Starting at 50, count forward:

6. 2 steps of 50.
7. 4 steps of 50.
8. 6 steps of 50.

How many steps of 50 are there:

9. between 0 and 200?
10. between 50 and 500?

Are the following true or false?

11. 150 is 4 steps of 50 from 0.
12. 200 is 2 steps of 50 from 50.
13. 250 is 3 steps of 50 from 100.

Starting at 350, count back:

14. 1 step of 50.
15. 3 steps of 50.

Set B

Starting at 0, count forward:

1. 2 steps of 50.
2. 5 steps of 50.
3. 7 steps of 50.

Starting at 100, count forward:

4. 3 steps of 50.
5. 6 steps of 50.
6. 8 steps of 50.

Complete these sentences with the correct number:

7. 350 is ☐ steps of 50 from 200.
8. 500 is ☐ steps of 50 from 50.
9. If you start at 850 and count back in steps of 50, which of these numbers do you get to?

   | 150 | 900 | 800 |
   | 240 | 360 | 400 |

10. Kyle has 400 cranberries. He needs 50 cranberries to make a pot of cranberry sauce. How many cranberries does he have left if he makes 5 pots?

11. Jamala starts at 350 and counts down 4 steps of 50. She then counts up 6 steps of 50. What number is she at now?

Set C

Starting at 400, count back:

1. 2 steps of 50.
2. 5 steps of 50.
3. 7 steps of 50.

How many steps of 50 are there:

4. between 200 and 450?
5. between 150 and 300?
6. between 400 and 750?

Find the missing numbers in each of these sequences:

7. ☐ 450 ☐ 550
8. ☐ ☐ 800 850

Starting at 250, count:

9. forward 7 steps of 50.
10. forward 11 steps of 50.
11. back 5 steps of 50.

Vinny has 550 grapevines. They are planted in rows of 50. How many grapevines will there be if:

12. 7 rows are added?
13. 2 rows are removed, then 5 are added?

14. Hazel has 800 grapevines. How many rows does Vinny need to plant to have the same number of grapevines as Hazel?

I can count in multiples of 50.

Counting in Multiples of 100

You can count in multiples of 100 by using the multiples of 10 — just remember to add an extra '0' to each number.

Examples

Starting at 0, count forward 3 steps of 100.

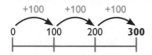

700 people go to see a pantomime. 4 groups of 100 people leave halfway through. How many people are left?

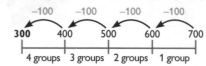

So there are **300 people** left.

Set A

Starting at 0, count forward:

1. 2 steps of 100.
2. 4 steps of 100.
3. 5 steps of 100.

Starting at 100, count forward:

4. 4 steps of 100.
5. 6 steps of 100.

Complete these sentences with the correct number:

6. 400 is ☐ steps of 100 from 0.
7. 600 is ☐ steps of 100 from 0.
8. 500 is ☐ steps of 100 from 200.

How many steps of 100 are there:

9. between 100 and 800?
10. between 200 and 900?

Starting at 700, count back:

11. 1 step of 100.
12. 5 steps of 100.
13. 7 steps of 100.

Set B

Starting at 0, count forward:

1. 3 steps of 100.
2. 7 steps of 100.
3. 8 steps of 100.

Starting at 200, count forward:

4. 2 steps of 100.
5. 5 steps of 100.
6. 8 steps of 100.

Starting at 800, count back:

7. 1 step of 100.
8. 2 steps of 100.
9. 5 steps of 100.

Find the missing numbers in each of these sequences:

10. ☐ 300 ☐ 500
11. 600 ☐ 800 ☐

12. Fabric comes in 100 cm rolls. Miranda has 500 cm of fabric and buys 4 more rolls. How much fabric does she have now?

13. Hugo needs to bake 600 gingerbread men. He's baked 2 batches of 100 so far. How many gingerbread men does he have left to bake?

Set C

Find the missing numbers in each of these sequences:

1. ☐ 400 ☐ 200
2. 800 ☐ ☐ 500

Starting at 900, count back:

3. 3 steps of 100.
4. 4 steps of 100.
5. 9 steps of 100.

How many steps of 100 are there:

6. between 100 and 500?
7. between 200 and 800?
8. between 100 and 1000?

Are the following true or false?

9. 600 is 3 steps of 100 from 300.
10. 200 is 6 steps of 100 from 800.
11. 1000 is 2 steps of 100 from 900.

12. A fisherman catches 700 fish and puts them in boxes of 100. He sells 2 boxes. How many fish are left?

13. Lucy and Ore are playing pool. They get 100 points for potting a ball. Lucy has 800 points and Ore has 300. How many balls does Ore need to pot to equal Lucy's score?

I can count in multiples of 100.

Number and Place Value — Review 2

Which number is each arrow pointing to?

(1)

(2)

(3)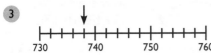

(4)

Copy the number line below.

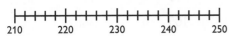

Draw and label an arrow pointing to:

(5) 222

(6) two hundred and sixteen

(7) two hundred and thirty-four

Estimate the number that each arrow is pointing to:

(8)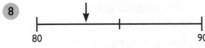

(9)

(10)

Starting at 0, count forward:

(11) 6 steps of 4.

(13) 9 steps of 4.

(12) 8 steps of 4.

(14) 12 steps of 4.

How many steps of 4 are there between:

(15) 0 and 32?

(17) 16 and 40?

(16) 4 and 28?

(18) 36 and 52?

(19) Jeremy is building some go-karts. Each go-kart has 4 wheels. He has used 36 wheels so far. He builds another 4 go-karts. How many wheels has he used now?

Starting at 8, count forward:

(20) 2 steps of 8.

(22) 8 steps of 8.

(21) 5 steps of 8.

(23) 10 steps of 8.

Are the following true or false?

(24) 16 is 1 step of 8 from 8.

(25) 32 is 3 steps of 8 from 16.

(26) 48 is 5 steps of 8 from 8.

(27) Helen is playing a board game. She gets 8 points when she lands on a blue square. She has 56 points, then lands on 3 more blue squares. How many points does she have now?

Starting at 0, count forward:

(28) 3 steps of 50.

(30) 9 steps of 50.

(29) 6 steps of 50.

(31) 11 steps of 50.

Complete each sentence with the correct number:

(32) 100 is ☐ steps of 50 from 0.

(33) 250 is ☐ steps of 50 from 50.

(34) 600 is ☐ steps of 50 from 100.

(35) The length of a swimming pool is 50 m. Ramesh swims 400 m, then swims another 5 lengths of the pool. How far did he swim in total?

Starting at 100, count forward:

(36) 2 steps of 100.

(38) 7 steps of 100.

(37) 5 steps of 100.

(39) 9 steps of 100.

Are the following true or false?

(40) 300 is 3 steps of 100 from 100.

(41) 700 is 6 steps of 100 from 100.

(42) 800 is 5 steps of 100 from 200.

(43) Three runners are doing laps of a 100 m track. Alf runs 600 m. Jed runs 2 more laps than Alf. Alexa runs 4 fewer laps than Jed. How far did Alexa run?

Give yourself a round of applause for showing these questions who's boss!

Counting 10 Up and Down

When you're counting up and down in 10s, remember that the ones digit doesn't change.

Examples

Write the number that is 10 more than 270.

+1 ten

2<u>7</u>0 → **2<u>8</u>0**

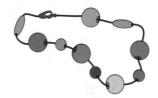

Maria buys a box of 542 beads. She uses 10 beads to make a bracelet. How many beads are left in the box?

−1 ten

5<u>4</u>2 → **5<u>3</u>2**

So there are **532 beads** left.

Set A

Write the number that is:

1. 10 more than 25
2. 10 more than 64
3. 10 less than 91
4. 10 more than 220
5. 10 less than 350
6. 10 less than 780

Which number is 10 more than:

7. forty-seven?
8. one hundred and thirty?
9. three hundred and eighty?

Which number is 10 less than:

10. five hundred and nineteen?
11. six hundred and forty-two?

12. Match the numbers which have a difference of 10.

47	273
283	119
109	368
62	57
358	72

Set B

Write the number that is:

1. 10 less than 37
2. 10 more than 81
3. 10 more than 280
4. 10 less than 438
5. 10 less than 502
6. 10 more than 697

Count in steps of 10 to find the missing numbers in each sequence:

7. 176 ☐ 196 ☐
8. ☐ 215 205 ☐

Which two numbers are:

9. 10 away from 473?
10. 2 steps of 10 away from 591?

11. A garden centre has 706 tomato plants. Kieran buys 10. How many tomato plants are left?

12. A bookcase has 148 books. A librarian adds 4 boxes of 10 books. How many books are there now?

Set C

Write the number that is:

1. 10 less than 359
2. 10 more than 614
3. 10 more than 799
4. 10 more than five hundred and twenty-eight
5. 10 less than eight hundred and one

Complete the sequences.

6. ☐ 493 ☐ 513
7. 726 716 ☐ ☐

Which two numbers are:

8. 10 away from 302?
9. 3 steps of 10 away from 262?
10. 5 steps of 10 away from 574?

Rico and his friends are playing a game. Rico has 391 points. Work out how many points each of his friends have:

11. Anna has 10 less than Rico.
12. Brian has 10 more than Rico.
13. Niles has 10 less than Anna.
14. Leah has 10 more than Brian.

I can count 10 up or down from any number.

Counting 100 Up and Down

Counting up in 100s is like counting up in 10s, but this time you're changing the hundreds digit. The tens and ones digits stay the same.

Examples

Write the number that is 100 less than 438.

−1 hundred

438 → **338**

There are 680 tadpoles in a pond. 100 more tadpoles hatch. How many tadpoles are there now?

+1 hundred

680 → **780**

So there are **780 tadpoles**.

Set A

Write the number that is:

1. 100 more than 162
2. 100 less than 230
3. 100 more than 378
4. 100 less than 459
5. 100 less than 611
6. 100 more than 820

7. Match the numbers which have a difference of 100.

102	286
391	557
457	202
186	291

Count in 100s to find the missing number in each of the sequences:

8. 195 295 ☐
9. ☐ 488 388
10. 967 867 ☐
11. ☐ 793 693
12. 612 712 ☐

Set B

Write the number that is:

1. 100 less than 263
2. 100 more than 475
3. 100 less than 582
4. 100 more than 636
5. 100 more than 884
6. 100 less than 971

Write the number that is:

7. 100 more than five hundred
8. 100 less than three hundred and forty-one
9. 100 more than seven hundred and sixty-seven
10. 100 less than eight hundred and ninety-nine

11. If you keep adding 100 to 172, which of these numbers do you get to?

72	372	984	672

12. A golfer has 249 golf tees. She buys 3 more packs of 100 tees. How many tees does she have now?

Set C

Write the number that is:

1. 100 more than 673
2. 100 more than 900
3. 100 less than 192
4. 100 more than four hundred and sixteen
5. 100 less than seven hundred and twenty-two

6. Carli has £956. She buys 3 plane tickets for £100 each. How much money does she have left?

Jeb has 689 building blocks. How many would he have if:

7. he got another box of 100 building blocks?
8. he gave 3 boxes of 100 building blocks to his friend?

A burger bar sold 332 hamburgers. It also sold:

- 100 fewer veggie burgers than hamburgers.
- 100 fewer Mexican burgers than veggie burgers.

How many:

9. veggie burgers did it sell?
10. Mexican burgers did it sell?

I can count 100 up or down from any number.

  ✓   ✓   ✓

x

Solving Number Problems

It's time to put what you've learnt to the test with some number problems — they cover everything you've seen in this section. Take a look at the examples first — they'll show you how to answer some of the questions.

Examples

The thermometer below records the temperature inside a pizza oven.

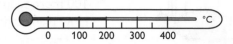

The temperature needs to be at 400 °C. How many steps of 50 °C does the temperature need to rise?

So the temperature needs to rise **4 steps** of 50 °C.

There are 378 parrots in a rainforest.
Two more flocks of 100 parrots arrive in the rainforest.

How many are there now?

So there are now **578 parrots**.

Set A

A researcher is measuring the heights of some trees. She puts her results into these tables:

Tree	Height
A	83 m
B	52 m

Tree	Height
C	65 m
D	42 m

1. Put the trees in order, starting with the shortest.

2. Which two trees have heights with a difference of 10 m?

3. Tree E is 55 m tall. Tree F is 73 m tall. Write these heights using words.

At a dog show, all the dogs have 4 legs.

4. Jo counts 12 legs in the small dogs event. 1 more dog is added to the event. How many legs are there now?

5. Kim counts 28 legs in the large dogs event. 2 dogs leave the event. How many legs are there now?

6. First place wins £617. The prize money decreases by £100 with each place. How much money does second place win?

7. The temperature in a garden is 13 °C. The temperature in a kitchen is 10 °C warmer than the garden. What is the temperature in the kitchen?

Each apple tree in an orchard produces 50 apples.

8. Donna picks 250 apples. Eric picks apples from 2 more trees than Donna. How many apples has Eric picked?

9. Reece has picked apples from 3 fewer trees than Donna. How many has Reece picked?

A beekeeper has 8 jars of honey. He collects 8 more jars each month. How many will he have in:

10. 3 months?

11. 5 months?

Quentin counts 523 buttercups in a field.

12. There are 100 fewer daisies than buttercups. How many daisies are there?

13. There are 100 more dandelions than buttercups. How many dandelions are there?

Set B

A race track has obstacles at different distances from the start line.

1. There is a sharp bend at 143 m. What is the value of the number in the tens position?

2. There is a muddy puddle at 278 m. Partition this amount into hundreds, tens and ones.

3. There is a flag 10 m before the finish line. If the flag is at 356 m, where is the finish line?

A charity is holding a raffle to raise money. The following four raffle tickets win the top prizes:

| 465 | 505 | 490 | 515 |

4. Copy out the number line below and use an arrow to mark on each raffle ticket number.

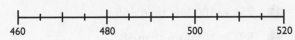

5. Tickets 492 and 503 also win a prize. Put all the raffle tickets in order from largest to smallest.

6. Write the smallest and the largest winning ticket numbers using words.

7. In April, 762 visitors went to see a volcano. There were 100 more visitors in May than in April. How many visitors were there in May?

Dhara is looking at the populations of different villages. Rewrite these populations using digits:

8. Four hundred and fifty-nine people

9. Six hundred and sixty-seven people

One village had a population of 981 people.

10. Partition this village's population into hundreds and a two-digit number.

It takes Moira 4 minutes to walk a lap of the park. She has already walked for 32 minutes. How many minutes will she have walked if she does:

11. 3 more laps?

12. 10 more laps?

13. Apples come in packs of 8. A shop has 96 apples. They sell 4 packs. How many apples are left in the shop?

Set C

1. A spoonful of sugar weighs 8 g. Lukas has a bowl of 64 g of sugar. How much sugar will be in the bowl if he removes 5 spoonfuls?

2. Priya is climbing a mountain which is 750 m tall. She is 400 m up the mountain. How many steps of 50 m does she need to climb to reach the top?

3. Here are some number cards:

| 3 | 9 | 1 | 5 | 6 | 4 |

Jack uses 3 of the cards to make a number. Use these clues to work out Jack's number:

- The hundreds digit is more than 7.
- The tens digit is a multiple of 4.
- The ones digit is 10 less than 16.

A pair of glasses costs £100.
A pair of sunglasses costs £50.

4. Georgina had £600 and bought two pairs of glasses. How much did she have left?

5. Karl spent £400 on a holiday and bought 3 pairs of sunglasses. How much did he spend in total?

The tables below show the number of pets a pet shop has sold since it opened.

Pet	Number	Pet	Number
Budgie	383	Rabbit	748
Python	260	Canary	579
Hamster	991	Parrot	416

6. Write all 6 pets in order, starting with the pet which was sold the least.

7. Partition the even numbers of pets into hundreds, tens and ones.

8. Rewrite the odd numbers of pets using words.

Some pupils make this timeline for history class:

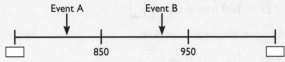

9. Estimate the years that Event A and Event B happened in.

10. Copy and complete the timeline.

Number and Place Value — Review 3

Which number is:

(1) 10 less than 41? (4) 10 less than 249?

(2) 10 more than 78? (5) 10 more than 395?

(3) 10 more than 122? (6) 10 less than 608?

Find the missing numbers:

(7) ☐ is 10 more than 36

(8) 78 is 10 less than ☐

(9) ☐ is 10 less than 249

(10) 565 is 10 more than ☐

(11) 791 is 10 less than ☐

(12) ☐ is 10 more than 894

(13) Working from left to right, match the numbers which have a difference of 10. The first one has been done for you.

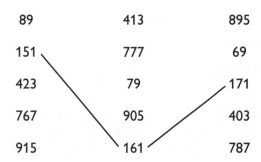

89	413	895
151	777	69
423	79	171
767	905	403
915	161	787

Which number is:

(14) 100 less than 165? (17) 100 less than 524?

(15) 100 more than 179? (18) 100 more than 685?

(16) 100 more than 331? (19) 100 more than 749?

Find the missing numbers:

(20) 237 is 100 more than ☐

(21) ☐ is 100 less than 458

(22) 691 is 100 less than ☐

(23) ☐ is 100 more than 823

(24) ☐ is 100 less than 846

(25) 1010 is 100 more than ☐

Start at 537 and count each of the steps below:

(26) down 1 step of 10.

(27) up 1 step of 100.

(28) up 2 steps of 10.

(29) down 4 steps of 100.

(30) up 5 steps of 10.

Are the following true or false?

(31) 43 is 10 less than 53

(32) 197 is 100 more than 297

(33) 256 is 100 less than 365

(34) 597 is 10 more than 587

(35) 943 is 100 more than 843

(36) 990 is 10 less than 1010

A container can hold 50 litres of custard.

(37) A factory uses 3 containers of custard to make some trifles. Count up in 50s to work out how many litres of custard the factory has used.

(38) A fridge had 500 litres of custard. 5 containers of custard were removed. How much was left in the fridge?

Lucy has 675 toy race cars.
Michael has 617 and Jonah has 639.

(39) Who has the most cars?

(40) Partition Lucy's number of toy race cars into hundreds, tens and ones.

This number line shows the distance an otter swims from one side of a river to the other.

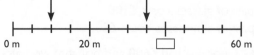

(41) Find the missing distance on the number line.

(42) Each arrow shows where the otter caught a fish. How far had the otter swum when it caught each fish?

Wow, look at all the questions you've just done — good job!

Number and Place Value — Challenges

1   Judy, Irina and Nick are playing dominoes. The number of dots on each half of a domino can be 1, 2, 3, 4, 5, 6, 7, 8 or 9. They each have 3 dominoes which are shown below.

Judy	Irina	Nick

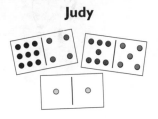   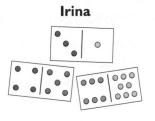   

On their first go, the total number of dots on the domino they play must be a multiple of 4.

a)   Draw the domino that each person can play on their first go.

b)   Draw some more dominoes that you could play on the first go. How many can you find?

2   This diagram below represents the number 342 using counters.

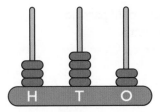

a)   What numbers do these diagrams represent?

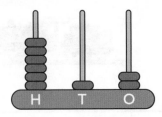   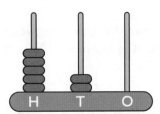   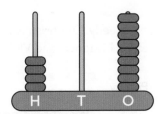

b)   Draw diagrams to show 813, 475 and 620.

c)   What is the smallest 3-digit number you can make with 17 counters?

d)   How many different 3-digit numbers can you make with 5 counters?

3   Look at these four number cards.

Use the cards to make a list of six different 3-digit numbers with:

a)   a 5 in the hundreds position.

b)   a 7 in the ones position.

c)   a 1 in the tens position.

d)   For each of your lists in parts a), b) and c), put the numbers in order starting with the smallest number.

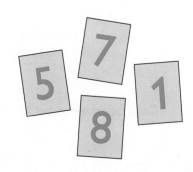

4   The 9-digit security code for a vault in a jewellery shop is made up from three 3-digit numbers.

a)   Use these clues to work out what each 3-digit number is:

- The first number is 4 steps of 50 forward from 500.

- The second number is 3 steps of 100 back from 440.

- The third number is 4 steps of 100 forward from 537.

b)   Now come up with your own 9-digit security code and
write some clues about the three 3-digit numbers.
Give your clues to a friend and see if they can crack your code.

5   Sanjay is coming up with different ways to partition the number 412.
So far he has come up with the list shown on the right.

a)   Which of Sanjay's partitions are correct?

b)   For each of the incorrect partitions,
change one number to make it correct.

c)   Can you think of five ways that you could partition
the number 648? Give your answers to
a friend to check if they are correct.

4 hundreds, 1 ten and 2 ones.

4 hundreds and 22 ones.

41 tens and 12 ones.

1 ten and 412 ones.

412 ones.

6   The Speedy Cumbrian is a steam train that travels between
Peachy Meadows and Violet Plains. The journey is 1000 miles.

Peachy
Meadows

Violet
Plains

0

1000

Clumsy Pete the train driver made this number line to plan his journey, but
he forgot to label some of the stations! Here is what he can remember:

Cauliflower Crag is 300 miles
after Peachy Meadows.

Pineapple Grove is halfway between
Peachy Meadows and Cauliflower Crag.

I know that Daffodil Flats is
400 miles before Violet Plains.

Strawberry Beach is 50 miles
before Daffodil Flats.

Copy out the number line, then use what Clumsy Pete remembers to add arrows pointing to each station.

7 Larry the llama wants to climb these hills to reach his favourite patch of grass.
The patches of grass on each hill are numbered.

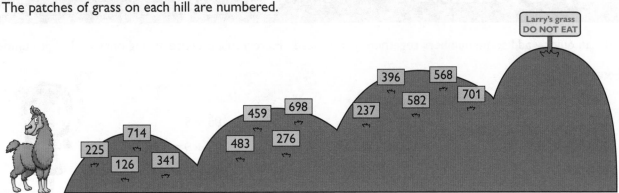

Larry's grass
DO NOT EAT

396   568
582   701
237
459   698
714   276
483
225
126   341

a) Write the numbers of the three patches Larry eats if he always eats the patch with:

   (i) the highest number on each hill?

   (ii) the smallest number on each hill?

   (iii) the largest digit in the tens place on each hill?

   (iv) the smallest digit in the ones place on each hill?

b) The patch of grass on the highest hill has lost its number.
Use these clues to find the patch number:

   • The digit in the hundreds place is odd and more than seven.

   • If you start at 100 and count up in steps of 50 you get to the patch number.

   • The digit in the tens place is not 0.

8 Oskar and Grant travel the world digging up dinosaur bones.
The fossil pits below represent how many bones they've found on different continents.

Key

Red Bones = 100

Green bones = 10

Yellow bones = 1

AFRICA

EUROPE

NORTH AMERICA

a) How many bones did they find on each continent?

They found 593 dinosaur bones in Asia and 487 in South America.

b) Draw a fossil pit for each of these continents — make sure the colours match the other fossil pits.

c) Put the five continents in order of the number of dinosaur bones found.
Start with the continent where they found the most dinosaur bones.

d) Think of your own 3-digit numbers and draw a fossil pit to represent each one.
Give your fossil pits to a friend and see if they can work out which number each one represents.

You've done an excellent job of tackling these tough challenges — give yourself a pat on the back!

Mental Addition — 1

You can quickly add some numbers together in your head. Here you'll practise adding ones to 3-digit numbers.

Examples

Work out the following in your head:

200 + 7   116 + 3   285 + 9

20<u>0</u> + <u>7</u> = **207**   1<u>16</u> + <u>3</u> = **119**   2<u>85</u> + <u>9</u> = **294**

(<u>0</u> + <u>7</u> = <u>7</u>)   (<u>16</u> + <u>3</u> = <u>19</u>)   (<u>85</u> + <u>9</u> = <u>94</u>)

Set A

Work out these in your head:

1. 100 + 0
2. 200 + 3
3. 500 + 8
4. 110 + 5
5. 320 + 6
6. 740 + 4

Work out these in your head:

7. 117 + 1
8. 206 + 3
9. 422 + 5
10. 213 + 4
11. 611 + 7
12. 805 + 2

Find the missing numbers:

13. 110 + ☐ = 119
14. 370 + ☐ = 376
15. 930 + ☐ = 931
16. 254 + ☐ = 259
17. 788 + ☐ = 789
18. 463 + ☐ = 467

Set B

Work out these in your head:

1. 193 + 6
2. 482 + 5
3. 928 + 0
4. 786 + 3
5. 291 + 7
6. 345 + 4

Work out these in your head:

7. 105 + 8
8. 567 + 6
9. 682 + 9
10. 848 + 7
11. 739 + 5
12. 437 + 4

Find the missing numbers:

13. 241 + ☐ = 248
14. 534 + ☐ = 537
15. 627 + ☐ = 629
16. 174 + ☐ = 183
17. 303 + ☐ = 311
18. 956 + ☐ = 962

Set C

Work out these in your head:

1. 129 + 0
2. 482 + 9
3. 517 + 5
4. 964 + 8
5. 283 + 7
6. 755 + 6

Work out these in your head:

7. 591 + 3 + 1
8. 693 + 4 + 2
9. 899 + 1 + 5
10. 397 + 4 + 6
11. 496 + 7 + 1
12. 198 + 9 + 5

Find the missing numbers:

13. 331 + ☐ = 340
14. 676 + ☐ = 684
15. 805 + ☐ = 811
16. 292 + ☐ = 301
17. 794 + ☐ = 803
18. 195 + ☐ = 202

I can add 3-digit numbers and ones.

Mental Addition — 2

Now it's time to have a go adding tens to 3-digit numbers.
Think about the place value of each digit and you'll fly through these questions.

Examples

Work out the following in your head:

300 + 10

$\underline{30}0 + \underline{1}0 = \mathbf{310}$

$(\underline{30} + \underline{1} = \underline{31})$

420 + 40

$\underline{42}0 + \underline{4}0 = \mathbf{460}$

$(\underline{42} + \underline{4} = \underline{46})$

372 + 90

$\underline{37}2 + \underline{9}0 = \mathbf{462}$

$(\underline{37} + \underline{9} = \underline{46})$

Set A

Work out these in your head:

1. 100 + 50
2. 200 + 40
3. 800 + 10
4. 400 + 20
5. 600 + 70
6. 700 + 90

Work out these in your head:

7. 110 + 30
8. 550 + 10
9. 340 + 50
10. 924 + 20
11. 861 + 10
12. 633 + 60

Find the missing numbers:

13. 300 + ☐ = 360
14. 500 + ☐ = 530
15. 900 + ☐ = 980
16. 270 + ☐ = 290
17. 422 + ☐ = 452
18. 715 + ☐ = 755

Set B

Work out these in your head:

1. 310 + 80
2. 540 + 30
3. 220 + 60
4. 719 + 10
5. 408 + 90
6. 962 + 20

Work out these in your head:

7. 670 + 40
8. 180 + 50
9. 490 + 50
10. 876 + 30
11. 533 + 70
12. 261 + 50

Find the missing numbers:

13. 910 + ☐ = 920
14. 720 + ☐ = 770
15. 830 + ☐ = 860
16. 144 + ☐ = 204
17. 385 + ☐ = 435
18. 627 + ☐ = 717

Set C

Work out these in your head:

1. 551 + 40
2. 827 + 30
3. 928 + 60
4. 116 + 90
5. 270 + 30
6. 690 + 20

Work out these in your head:

7. 312 + 60 + 20
8. 406 + 70 + 30
9. 783 + 30 + 10
10. 159 + 80 + 50
11. 592 + 40 + 30
12. 874 + 30 + 20

Find the missing numbers:

13. 932 + ☐ = 952
14. 339 + ☐ = 389
15. 720 + ☐ = 810
16. 150 + ☐ = 220
17. 863 + 30 + ☐ = 913
18. 293 + 20 + ☐ = 383

I can add 3-digit numbers and tens.

Mental Addition — 3

Adding big numbers together in your head doesn't need to be scary
— keep thinking about place value to add hundreds to 3-digit numbers.

Examples

Work out the following in your head:

100 + 100

100 + 100 = **200**

(1 + 1 = 2)

610 + 200

610 + 200 = **810**

(6 + 2 = 8)

102 + 200 + 300

102 + 200 + 300 = **602**

(1 + 2 + 3 = 6)

Set A

Work out these in your head:

1. 200 + 100
2. 500 + 300
3. 800 + 100
4. 300 + 400
5. 100 + 600
6. 700 + 200

Work out these in your head:

7. 410 + 200
8. 660 + 300
9. 740 + 100
10. 270 + 500
11. 120 + 400
12. 380 + 300

Find the missing numbers:

13. 200 + ☐ = 500
14. 500 + ☐ = 600
15. 400 + ☐ = 900
16. 310 + ☐ = 410
17. 670 + ☐ = 870
18. 430 + ☐ = 830

Set B

Work out these in your head:

1. 170 + 800
2. 530 + 400
3. 650 + 200
4. 490 + 400
5. 760 + 200
6. 140 + 300

Work out these in your head:

7. 549 + 100
8. 283 + 200
9. 671 + 300
10. 168 + 700
11. 305 + 400
12. 284 + 500

Find the missing numbers:

13. 840 + ☐ = 940
14. 560 + ☐ = 760
15. 432 + ☐ = 932
16. 386 + ☐ = 686
17. 677 + ☐ = 777
18. 300 + ☐ = 1000

Set C

Work out these in your head:

1. 392 + 500
2. 429 + 200
3. 387 + 300
4. 163 + 400
5. 395 + 600
6. 208 + 700

Work out these in your head:

7. 243 + 200 + 400
8. 391 + 400 + 100
9. 314 + 200 + 100
10. 357 + 200 + 200
11. 432 + 200 + 300
12. 196 + 100 + 300

Find the missing numbers:

13. 581 + ☐ = 981
14. 206 + ☐ = 806
15. 198 + ☐ = 298
16. 586 + 300 + ☐ = 986
17. 311 + 100 + ☐ = 811
18. 600 + 200 + ☐ = 1000

I can add 3-digit numbers and hundreds.

Mental Addition Methods

There are a few different methods that you can choose from for adding trickier numbers together in your head.

Examples

Work out the following in your head:

334 + 52

= 334 + 50 + 2 ← Partition the number into tens and ones.

= 384 + 2 = **386**

626 + 49 ← Add on a near multiple of 10 first.

= 626 + 50 − 1

= 676 − 1 = **675**

Count up to an easier number and then add on the rest.

194 + 18

= 194 + 6 + 12

= 200 + 12 = **212**

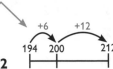

Set A

Use partitioning to work out:

1. 64 + 32
2. 27 + 51
3. 130 + 42
4. 250 + 33
5. 200 + 120
6. 450 + 240

Use near multiples of 10 to work out:

7. 54 + 39
8. 43 + 49
9. 52 + 99
10. 108 + 69
11. 134 + 59
12. 312 + 79

Work these out by counting up:

13. 68 + 27
14. 47 + 36
15. 58 + 34
16. 96 + 58
17. 193 + 28
18. 188 + 74

Set B

Use partitioning to work out:

1. 230 + 47
2. 362 + 35
3. 520 + 350

Work these out by counting up:

4. 94 + 68
5. 193 + 48
6. 695 + 27

Use near multiples of 10 to work out:

7. 113 + 79
8. 724 + 69
9. 832 + 99

Choose a method to work out:

10. 597 + 85
11. 335 + 59
12. 420 + 132

Find the missing numbers:

13. 30 + ☐ + 5 = 75
14. 150 + 20 + ☐ = 173
15. 240 + ☐ + 8 = 298
16. 347 + ☐ + 2 = 379
17. 231 + 20 + ☐ = 256
18. 124 + 60 + ☐ = 187
19. 180 + ☐ + 8 = 488

Set C

Use partitioning to work out:

1. 340 + 150
2. 624 + 270
3. 365 + 320
4. 480 + 109
5. 351 + 202
6. 563 + 225

Find the missing numbers:

7. 530 + 300 + ☐ = 880
8. 321 + 300 + 40 + ☐ = 667
9. 460 + 140 + ☐ = 618
10. 642 + 58 + ☐ = 721
11. 263 + ☐ + 1 = 324
12. 358 + 60 + ☐ = 423

Choose a method to work out:

13. 153 + 39
14. 143 + 54
15. 196 + 77
16. 398 + 46
17. 455 + 69
18. 270 + 420

I can do mental addition using different methods.

Addition and Subtraction — Review 1

Work out these in your head:

1) 300 + 8
2) 400 + 7
3) 130 + 2
4) 580 + 0
5) 940 + 6
6) 161 + 7
7) 216 + 3
8) 783 + 5
9) 385 + 8
10) 729 + 6
11) 914 + 9
12) 895 + 6
13) 391 + 3 + 5
14) 168 + 7 + 4

Find the missing numbers in these calculations:

15) 800 + ☐ = 804
16) 620 + ☐ = 621
17) 550 + ☐ = 559
18) 835 + ☐ = 837
19) 439 + ☐ = 446
20) 106 + ☐ = 112
21) 393 + ☐ = 401

Work out these in your head:

22) 100 + 20
23) 800 + 30
24) 930 + 50
25) 240 + 40
26) 480 + 10
27) 548 + 20
28) 721 + 60
29) 419 + 70
30) 790 + 50
31) 280 + 30
32) 360 + 60
33) 486 + 20
34) 832 + 40 + 20
35) 674 + 30 + 50

Find the missing numbers in these calculations:

36) 500 + ☐ = 510
37) 120 + ☐ = 160
38) 310 + ☐ = 370
39) 435 + ☐ = 475
40) 902 + ☐ = 992
41) 830 + ☐ = 910
42) 750 + ☐ = 820
43) 689 + ☐ = 759

Work out these in your head:

44) 400 + 200
45) 300 + 600
46) 900 + 100
47) 520 + 400
48) 130 + 600
49) 190 + 100
50) 562 + 300
51) 727 + 100
52) 561 + 200
53) 815 + 100

Work out these in your head:

54) 231 + 100 + 100
55) 392 + 200 + 100
56) 473 + 300 + 200
57) 159 + 200 + 500

Find the missing numbers in these calculations:

58) 200 + ☐ = 400
59) 160 + ☐ = 560
60) 470 + ☐ = 770
61) 573 + ☐ = 673
62) 145 + 300 + ☐ = 845
63) 519 + 200 + ☐ = 919

Choose the best method to work out:

64) 60 + 36
65) 94 + 28
66) 32 + 59
67) 280 + 35
68) 250 + 49
69) 300 + 140
70) 240 + 220
71) 798 + 47
72) 413 + 59
73) 245 + 320
74) 382 + 105
75) 253 + 399

Find the missing numbers in these calculations:

76) 90 + 40 + ☐ = 137
77) 23 + 60 + ☐ = 85
78) 450 + ☐ + 7 = 487
79) 472 + 300 + ☐ = 792
80) 377 + 20 + ☐ = 404
81) 346 + 200 + 30 + ☐ = 579

That was a lot of questions to answer — nice work!

Mental Subtraction — 1

Now let's try some mental subtraction. It's the same idea as with addition — you just have to remember to think about place value. Let's have a go at subtracting some ones from 3-digit numbers.

Examples

Work out the following in your head:

109 – 3	920 – 4	752 – 5
10<u>9</u> – <u>3</u> = **106**	9<u>20</u> – <u>4</u> = **916**	7<u>52</u> – <u>5</u> = **747**
(<u>9</u> – <u>3</u> = <u>6</u>)	(<u>20</u> – <u>4</u> = <u>16</u>)	(<u>52</u> – <u>5</u> = <u>47</u>)

Set A

Work out these in your head:

1. 604 – 3
2. 207 – 5
3. 806 – 1
4. 308 – 4
5. 719 – 8
6. 527 – 7

Work out these in your head:

7. 180 – 3
8. 420 – 1
9. 980 – 2
10. 230 – 6
11. 840 – 5
12. 390 – 3

Find the missing numbers:

13. 701 – ☐ = 700
14. 905 – ☐ = 903
15. 138 – ☐ = 132
16. 549 – ☐ = 547
17. 260 – ☐ = 253
18. 480 – ☐ = 477

Set B

Work out these in your head:

1. 209 – 7
2. 728 – 5
3. 200 – 2
4. 800 – 8
5. 920 – 3
6. 650 – 9

Work out these in your head:

7. 830 – 7
8. 190 – 4
9. 344 – 8
10. 473 – 4
11. 518 – 9
12. 172 – 6

Find the missing numbers:

13. 900 – ☐ = 896
14. 600 – ☐ = 592
15. 310 – ☐ = 303
16. 570 – ☐ = 568
17. 485 – ☐ = 479
18. 541 – ☐ = 532

Set C

Work out these in your head:

1. 409 – 8
2. 116 – 5
3. 500 – 7
4. 700 – 5
5. 345 – 7
6. 852 – 6

Work out these in your head:

7. 204 – 7
8. 601 – 3
9. 907 – 9
10. 722 – 2 – 4
11. 413 – 5 – 2
12. 156 – 7 – 3

Find the missing numbers:

13. 900 – ☐ = 899
14. 213 – ☐ = 207
15. 646 – ☐ = 639
16. 305 – ☐ = 297
17. 818 – 9 – ☐ = 802
18. 523 – ☐ – 8 = 512

I can subtract 3-digit numbers and ones.

Mental Subtraction — 2

Now have a go at subtracting tens from 3-digit numbers.
Nothing to worry about, just keep thinking about the place value of each digit.

Examples

Work out the following in your head:

170 – 30

1<u>7</u>0 – <u>3</u>0 = **140**

(<u>7</u> – <u>3</u> = <u>4</u>)

260 – 80

2<u>6</u>0 – <u>8</u>0 = **180**

(<u>26</u> – <u>8</u> = <u>18</u>)

590 – 20 – 50

<u>5</u>90 – <u>2</u>0 – <u>5</u>0 = **520**

(<u>59</u> – <u>2</u> – <u>5</u> = <u>52</u>)

Set A

Work out these in your head:

1. 290 – 60
2. 540 – 20
3. 750 – 40
4. 380 – 50
5. 860 – 30
6. 430 – 10

Work out these in your head:

7. 183 – 30
8. 657 – 50
9. 971 – 40
10. 818 – 10
11. 725 – 20
12. 294 – 70

Find the missing numbers:

13. 170 – ☐ = 150
14. 680 – ☐ = 610
15. 950 – ☐ = 910
16. 368 – ☐ = 328
17. 431 – ☐ = 401
18. 542 – ☐ = 512

Set B

Work out these in your head:

1. 670 – 40
2. 490 – 80
3. 128 – 10
4. 992 – 80
5. 283 – 20
6. 376 – 50

Work out these in your head:

7. 500 – 30
8. 400 – 70
9. 800 – 40
10. 210 – 20
11. 920 – 80
12. 160 – 90

Find the missing numbers:

13. 736 – ☐ = 706
14. 694 – ☐ = 634
15. 300 – ☐ = 210
16. 900 – ☐ = 820
17. 240 – ☐ = 170
18. 830 – ☐ = 790

Set C

Work out these in your head:

1. 790 – 70
2. 357 – 40
3. 570 – 80
4. 660 – 70
5. 410 – 50
6. 930 – 40

Work out these in your head:

7. 153 – 70
8. 813 – 30
9. 237 – 50
10. 764 – 20 – 10
11. 382 – 40 – 30
12. 409 – 20 – 40

Find the missing numbers:

13. 170 – ☐ = 80
14. 220 – ☐ = 150
15. 618 – ☐ = 578
16. 533 – ☐ = 453
17. 668 – ☐ – 30 = 618
18. 967 – 30 – ☐ = 887

I can subtract 3-digit numbers and tens.

Mental Subtraction — 3

This page gives you lots of practice taking hundreds away from 3-digit numbers.
You can still do it in your head by looking at the hundreds digit of each number.

Examples

Work out the following in your head:

$200 - 100$

$\underline{2}00 - \underline{1}00 = \mathbf{100}$

$(\underline{2} - \underline{1} = \underline{1})$

$710 - 200$

$\underline{7}10 - \underline{2}00 = \mathbf{510}$

$(\underline{7} - \underline{2} = \underline{5})$

$530 - 200 - 200$

$\underline{5}30 - \underline{2}00 - \underline{2}00 = \mathbf{130}$

$(\underline{5} - \underline{2} - \underline{2} = \underline{1})$

Set A

Work out these in your head:

1. $600 - 300$
2. $900 - 500$
3. $200 - 200$
4. $700 - 300$
5. $700 - 600$
6. $800 - 400$

Work out these in your head:

7. $350 - 200$
8. $790 - 400$
9. $840 - 300$
10. $410 - 200$
11. $560 - 300$
12. $620 - 500$

Find the missing numbers:

13. $900 - \boxed{} = 800$
14. $600 - \boxed{} = 400$
15. $500 - \boxed{} = 300$
16. $830 - \boxed{} = 530$
17. $790 - \boxed{} = 390$
18. $400 - \boxed{} = 0$

Set B

Work out these in your head:

1. $400 - 200$
2. $700 - 400$
3. $180 - 100$
4. $350 - 200$
5. $660 - 300$
6. $530 - 400$

Work out these in your head:

7. $272 - 200$
8. $826 - 500$
9. $957 - 700$
10. $413 - 300$
11. $594 - 200$
12. $735 - 500$

Find the missing numbers:

13. $300 - \boxed{} = 0$
14. $600 - \boxed{} = 200$
15. $780 - \boxed{} = 680$
16. $460 - \boxed{} = 160$
17. $923 - \boxed{} = 623$
18. $765 - \boxed{} = 365$

Set C

Work out these in your head:

1. $670 - 500$
2. $850 - 400$
3. $210 - 200$
4. $370 - 200$
5. $938 - 600$
6. $715 - 500$

Work out these in your head:

7. $384 - 200 - 100$
8. $571 - 200 - 200$
9. $792 - 300 - 100$
10. $827 - 400 - 200$
11. $629 - 300 - 200$
12. $978 - 400 - 300$

Find the missing numbers:

13. $380 - \boxed{} = 80$
14. $510 - \boxed{} = 210$
15. $274 - \boxed{} = 174$
16. $893 - \boxed{} = 593$
17. $963 - 400 - \boxed{} = 463$
18. $837 - 500 - \boxed{} = 37$

I can subtract 3-digit numbers and hundreds.

Mental Subtraction Methods

There's more than one way to subtract numbers in your head.
This page has got a few different methods for you to have a go at.

Examples

Work out the following in your head:

178 – 34

178 – 30 – 4 ← Partition the number into tens and ones.

= 148 – 4 = **144**

146 – 29 ← Subtract a near multiple of 10 first.

146 – 30 + 1

= 116 + 1 = **117**

Count up from the smaller number to the bigger one.

306 – 288

288 + 12 + 6 = 306

12 + 6 = **18**

So 306 – 288 = **18**.

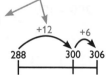

Set A

Use partitioning to work out:

1. 147 – 35
2. 265 – 43
3. 468 – 47
4. 370 – 150
5. 560 – 240
6. 402 – 201

Use near multiples of 10 to work out:

7. 74 – 39
8. 86 – 79
9. 93 – 59
10. 148 – 29
11. 187 – 69
12. 265 – 49

Work these out by counting up:

13. 53 – 45
14. 97 – 78
15. 64 – 46
16. 113 – 97
17. 203 – 187
18. 152 – 138

Set B

Use partitioning to work out:

1. 480 – 230
2. 730 – 520
3. 578 – 304

Work these out by counting up:

4. 105 – 82
5. 118 – 95
6. 207 – 196

Use near multiples of 10 to work out:

7. 190 – 79
8. 252 – 39
9. 656 – 49

Choose a method to work out:

10. 442 – 39
11. 685 – 240
12. 312 – 294

Find the missing numbers:

13. 70 – 40 – ☐ = 22
14. 264 – ☐ – 1 = 213
15. 748 – 300 – ☐ = 428
16. 480 – ☐ – 3 = 427
17. 590 – 50 – ☐ = 537
18. 346 – 100 – ☐ = 216
19. 459 – ☐ – 40 = 119

Set C

Use partitioning to work out:

1. 480 – 38
2. 750 – 45
3. 757 – 330
4. 623 – 410
5. 542 – 141
6. 483 – 109

Find the missing numbers:

7. 740 – 30 – ☐ = 702
8. 856 – 300 – ☐ = 553
9. 688 – ☐ – 40 = 248
10. 563 – 100 – 40 – ☐ = 421
11. 487 – 200 – ☐ = 227
12. 934 – 400 – 50 – ☐ = 483

Choose a method to work out:

13. 997 – 79
14. 678 – 450
15. 859 – 799
16. 736 – 59
17. 432 – 205
18. 903 – 887

I can do mental subtraction using different methods.

Addition and Subtraction — Review 2

Work out these in your head:

1. 102 – 1
2. 806 – 4
3. 549 – 7
4. 728 – 5
5. 100 – 6
6. 400 – 9
7. 470 – 2
8. 920 – 6
9. 793 – 7
10. 822 – 4
11. 204 – 8 – 3
12. 501 – 5 – 2

Find the missing numbers in these calculations:

13. 903 – ☐ = 901
14. 675 – ☐ = 671
15. 710 – ☐ = 703
16. 896 – ☐ = 888
17. 183 – ☐ = 174
18. 900 – 3 – ☐ = 892
19. 205 – 4 – ☐ = 199

Work out these in your head:

20. 790 – 40
21. 220 – 20
22. 860 – 50
23. 183 – 20
24. 842 – 10
25. 375 – 40
26. 500 – 50
27. 900 – 10
28. 180 – 90
29. 360 – 80
30. 820 – 50
31. 448 – 60
32. 639 – 20 – 40
33. 823 – 30 – 10

Find the missing numbers in these calculations:

34. 150 – ☐ = 120
35. 676 – ☐ = 646
36. 700 – ☐ = 680
37. 100 – ☐ = 70
38. 320 – ☐ = 270
39. 460 – 40 – ☐ = 390
40. 823 – 20 – ☐ = 753

Work out these in your head:

41. 800 – 600
42. 400 – 300
43. 700 – 200
44. 900 – 600
45. 190 – 100
46. 340 – 200
47. 580 – 400
48. 940 – 500
49. 158 – 100
50. 821 – 500
51. 347 – 200 – 100
52. 864 – 400 – 300

Find the missing numbers in these calculations:

53. 300 – ☐ = 100
54. 500 – ☐ = 200
55. 230 – ☐ = 130
56. 860 – ☐ = 360
57. 748 – ☐ = 448
58. 675 – 100 – ☐ = 275
59. 931 – 300 – ☐ = 131

Choose the best method to work out:

60. 87 – 52
61. 90 – 76
62. 60 – 49
63. 277 – 34
64. 568 – 59
65. 470 – 57
66. 520 – 78
67. 430 – 23
68. 405 – 384
69. 786 – 520
70. 487 – 298
71. 583 – 231
72. 541 – 492
73. 448 – 205

Find the missing numbers in these calculations:

74. 74 – 50 – ☐ = 21
75. 90 – 50 – ☐ = 31
76. 124 – 10 – ☐ = 113
77. 370 – 30 – ☐ = 332
78. 568 – 200 – ☐ = 318
79. 650 – 300 – ☐ = 342
80. 843 – 500 – 10 – ☐ = 324
81. 249 – 100 – 50 – ☐ = 91

Have a go at these questions and you'll be a super star at mental subtraction!

Written Addition — 1

You can work out additions by writing it down on paper instead of working it out in your head.
There are two different written methods you can use...

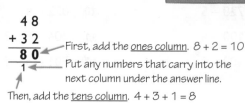

Examples

Answer the following:

62 + 11

```
    6 2
  + 1 1
  ─────
      3  ← First, add the ones. 2 + 1 = 3
  + 7 0  ← Then, add the tens. 60 + 10 = 70
  ─────
    7 3  ← Then add the columns together.
```

48 + 32

```
    4 8
  + 3 2
  ─────
    8 0  ← First, add the ones column. 8 + 2 = 10
    1    ← Put any numbers that carry into the
           next column under the answer line.
```

Then, add the tens column. 4 + 3 + 1 = 8

Set A

Work out the answers using one of the methods above:

(1)   2 3
    + 1 2

(2)   6 2
    + 2 4

(3)   8 6
    + 1 3

(4)   5 1
    + 4 7

(5)   3 1
    + 5 3

(6)   5 6
    + 3 3

(7)   5 7
    + 2 4

(8)   4 8
    + 3 5

(9)   2 9
    + 3 7

Answer the following:

(10) 43 + 46

(11) 72 + 27

(12) 38 + 41

(13) 35 + 27

(14) 62 + 19

(15) 46 + 28

Set B

Work out the answers:

(1)   3 8
    + 4 5

(2)   6 3
    + 2 7

(3)   3 4
    + 5 8

(4)   5 2
    + 5 4

(5)   6 6
    + 7 2

(6)   8 5
    + 3 4

Work out:

(7)   48 + 37

(8)   26 + 35

(9)   68 + 24

(10) 53 + 56

(11) 42 + 86

(12) 75 + 44

Find the number that is:

(13) 63 more than 28

(14) 34 more than 58

(15) 41 more than 86

(16) 38 more than 55

(17) 58 more than 61

(18) 76 more than 83

Set C

Work out:

(1)   9 5
    + 6 7

(2)   8 9
    + 4 3

(3)   5 6
    + 8 5

Work out:

(4)   58 + 91

(5)   85 + 23

(6)   74 + 59

(7)   37 + 83

(8)   65 + 58

(9)   32 + 99

Find the number that is:

(10) 46 more than 58

(11) 85 more than 35

(12) 74 more than 57

(13) 54 more than 76

(14) 92 more than 49

(15) 36 more than 77

The table shows how many badges 3 children have.

Ana	Ben	Cleo
35	78	69

How many do:

(16) Ana and Ben have?

(17) Ben and Cleo have?

(18) Cleo and Ana have?

I can do written addition with 2-digit numbers.

Written Addition — 2

You can use written methods to add 3-digit numbers too — take a look at the examples then give it a go.

Examples

Answer the following:

623 + 118

```
  6 2 3
+ 1 1 8
─────────
    1 1   ←── First, add the ones.  3 + 8 = 11
+   3 0   ←── Then, add the tens.  20 + 10 = 30
+ 7 0 0   ←── Then, add the hundreds.  600 + 100 = 700
─────────
  7 4 1   ←── Finally, add the columns together.
```

685 + 108

```
  6 8 5
+ 1 0 8
─────────
  7 9 3   ←── First, add the ones column.  5 + 8 = 13
  1       ←── Then, add the tens column.  8 + 0 + 1 = 9
```
Finally, add the hundreds column. 6 + 1 = 7

Set A

Work out the answers using one of the methods above:

1. 332 + 457
2. 728 + 261
3. 385 + 213
4. 462 + 136
5. 174 + 625
6. 237 + 452
7. 545 + 356
8. 603 + 278
9. 882 + 156

Work out:

10. 552 + 437
11. 710 + 273
12. 524 + 404
13. 154 + 237
14. 728 + 133
15. 483 + 334

Set B

Work out the answers:

1. 245 + 132
2. 583 + 216
3. 385 + 602
4. 254 + 337
5. 738 + 259
6. 173 + 596

Answer these:

7. 432 + 554
8. 757 + 241
9. 328 + 463
10. 659 + 236
11. 685 + 124
12. 280 + 537

Find the number that is:

13. 457 more than 362
14. 758 more than 161
15. 166 more than 452
16. 244 more than 348
17. 563 more than 228
18. 112 more than 394

Set C

Work out:

1. 265 + 326
2. 734 + 181
3. 328 + 653
4. 336 + 584
5. 215 + 587
6. 663 + 238

Answer these:

7. 583 + 231
8. 467 + 325
9. 296 + 387
10. 505 + 396
11. 738 + 476
12. 361 + 749

Last year Detective Dan solved 124 mysteries. Detective Dora solved 356 and Detective Dina solved 248.

How many mysteries did:

13. Dan and Dora solve?
14. Dina and Dora solve?
15. Dan and Dina solve?

I can do written addition with 3-digit numbers.

Written Addition — 3

Here are some trickier written addition questions, but you can always use the same methods...

Examples

Zara was writing a story. She wrote 459 words before lunch and 62 words after lunch. How many words did she write in total?

```
    4 5 9
  +   6 2
    5 2 1    So she wrote 521 words.
    1 1
```

Three friends are making daisy chains. Habib uses 203 daisies, Jack uses 162 and Spencer uses 98. How many daisies have they used in total?

```
    2 0 3
  + 1 6 2    ← Make sure you line up the
  +   9 8       digits in the correct columns.
    4 6 3    So they used 463 daisies.
    1 1
```

Set A

Work out the answers:

1.
```
    5 7 2
  +   2 6
```

2.
```
    7 2 3
  +   3 4
```

3.
```
    3 4 6
  +   4 8
```

4.
```
      3 2
  +   5 3
  +   1 3
```

5.
```
      4 9
  +   2 6
  +   2 2
```

Answer the following:

6. 826 + 43

7. 653 + 76

8. 732 + 49

9. 43 + 15 + 30

10. 41 + 25 + 21

11. 25 + 34 + 37

12. Willow got 128 marks on her English test. Ruby got 37 marks more than Willow. How many marks did Ruby get?

13. Seth has 18 crayons. His mum buys him 48 more and his sister gives him another 31. How many crayons does he have in total?

Set B

Work out the answers:

1.
```
    8 4 6
  +   3 5
```

2.
```
    7 4 2
  +   8 3
```

3.
```
    1 6 4
  +   5 8
```

4.
```
      2 3
  +   4 3
  +   1 7
```

5.
```
    3 4 5
  + 2 3 2
  + 1 5 1
```

Answer the following:

6. 502 + 35

7. 284 + 41

8. 453 + 59

9. 108 + 67

10. 21 + 73 + 95

11. 108 + 238 + 123

12. George has 376 fish in his pond. He adds another 47 fish. How many fish are there in the pond now?

13. Raisa has 65 books, Danny has 82 books and Masie has 31 books. How many books do they have in total?

Set C

Work out:

1.
```
    6 3 2
  +   8 4
```

2.
```
    2 5 4
  +   6 8
```

3.
```
    4 7 3
  +   4 7
```

4.
```
    4 2 2
  + 1 4 3
  + 2 6 2
```

5.
```
    2 6 4
  + 1 2 8
  +   1 2
```

Answer the following:

6. 753 + 75

7. 695 + 87

8. 738 + 63

9. 157 + 354 + 373

10. 388 + 43 + 21

11. 542 + 135 + 32

12. Tony scored 247 points in a game and got an 88 point bonus. How many points did he get in total?

13. Flavia connected 257 jigsaw pieces. She had 56 edge pieces and 194 middle pieces left. How many jigsaw pieces are there in total?

I am confident doing addition using written methods.

Addition and Subtraction — Review 3

Work out:

1. 36
    +42

2. 73
    +25

3. 58
    +37

4. 74
    +16

5. 67
    +72

6. 45
    +93

7. 48
    +74

8. 86
    +25

Use a written method to work out:

9. 51 + 36

10. 75 + 24

11. 47 + 31

12. 48 + 39

13. 64 + 27

14. 39 + 45

15. 65 + 73

16. 84 + 41

17. 76 + 42

18. 57 + 73

19. 95 + 27

20. 78 + 43

Work out:

21. 362
    +427

22. 847
    +152

23. 426
    +365

24. 746
    +237

25. 373
    +254

26. 648
    +193

27. 745
    +358

28. 484
    +839

Use a written method to work out:

29. 342 + 436

30. 274 + 515

31. 735 + 247

32. 538 + 354

33. 273 + 372

34. 184 + 552

35. 638 + 421

36. 363 + 925

37. 482 + 249

38. 538 + 273

39. 645 + 507

40. 428 + 943

Work out:

41. 846
    + 32

42. 738
    + 27

43. 482
    + 36

44. 168
    + 25

45. 563
    + 28

46. 653
    + 64

Use a written method to work out:

47. 746 + 53

48. 534 + 45

49. 773 + 42

50. 273 + 34

51. 948 + 71

52. 636 + 84

Work out:

53. 23
    +41
    +14

54. 48
    +74
    +27

55. 247
    + 45
    + 32

56. 308
    +254
    + 46

Use a written method to work out:

57. 54 + 32 + 24

58. 73 + 23 + 45

59. 176 + 134 + 223

60. 456 + 34 + 52

61. 456 + 321 + 43

62. 309 + 421 + 62

63. Millie the dog trampled 103 flowers on Saturday and 68 flowers on Sunday. How many flowers did she trample in total?

64. In a school council election, Janko got 82 votes, Zack got 74 votes and Nia got 56 votes. How many people voted for Janko, Zack and Nia?

65. It took Kevin 3 days to build a wall. On the first day he laid 304 bricks, on the second day he laid 192 bricks and on the third day he laid 86 bricks. How many bricks did he lay in total?

You're doing great — good job!

Written Subtraction — 1

You might want to subtract numbers on paper rather than in your head. Here are two ways you can do it...

Examples

Work out: 53 – 27

27 = 20 + 7

```
    5 3
  –   7   ←──── First subtract 7.
  ─────
    4 6
  – 2 0   ←──── Then subtract 20.
  ─────
    2 6
```

What is 92 – 44?

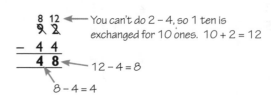

```
    8 12
    ⁹ ²   ←──── You can't do 2 – 4, so 1 ten is
              exchanged for 10 ones.  10 + 2 = 12
  – 4 4
  ─────
    4 8   ←──── 12 – 4 = 8
          ↖
          8 – 4 = 4
```

Set A

Work out the answers using one of the methods above:

1)
```
  9 5
– 3 2
```

2)
```
  6 7
– 4 5
```

3)
```
  8 2
– 6 1
```

4)
```
  7 8
– 4 7
```

5)
```
  5 4
– 3 3
```

6)
```
  9 8
– 8 4
```

7)
```
  5 4
– 3 2
```

8)
```
  7 8
– 2 1
```

9)
```
  6 7
– 1 4
```

Work out:

10) 39 – 18

11) 58 – 23

12) 72 – 41

13) 46 – 25

14) 84 – 42

15) 95 – 44

Set B

Work out the answers:

1)
```
  5 7
– 3 6
```

2)
```
  7 4
– 2 2
```

3)
```
  9 3
– 4 1
```

4)
```
  8 6
– 6 8
```

5)
```
  5 4
– 2 6
```

6)
```
  7 1
– 5 2
```

Work out:

7) 94 – 33

8) 38 – 27

9) 76 – 45

10) 64 – 37

11) 52 – 18

12) 73 – 38

Find the number that is:

13) 52 less than 84

14) 34 less than 76

15) 62 less than 85

16) 47 less than 93

17) 29 less than 68

18) 84 less than 93

Set C

Work out:

1)
```
  7 3
– 2 2
```

2)
```
  9 8
– 4 9
```

3)
```
  6 2
– 5 4
```

Work out:

4) 98 – 38

5) 84 – 42

6) 65 – 48

7) 74 – 27

8) 52 – 38

9) 77 – 59

Find the number that is:

10) 71 less than 94

11) 63 less than 86

12) 39 less than 64

13) 26 less than 54

14) 49 less than 86

15) 58 less than 73

16) Faizel is 98 years old. Kiara is 45 years younger than Faizel. How old is Kiara?

17) Joel counted 76 blue cars and 58 green cars on the way to school. How many fewer green cars than blue cars did he count?

I can do written subtraction with 2-digit numbers.

Written Subtraction — 2

Now let's have a go at subtracting some 3-digit numbers. Don't worry, just use the same methods as before.

Examples

What is 452 − 136?

136 = 100 + 30 + 6

```
    4 5 2
  −     6   ← First subtract 6.
    4 4 6
  −   3 0   ← Then subtract 30.
    4 1 6
  − 1 0 0   ← Then subtract 100.
    3 1 6
```

Work out 645 − 338.

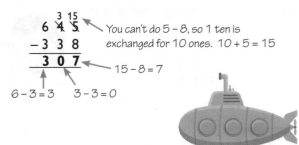

```
      3 15
    6 ̶4 ̶5   ← You can't do 5 − 8, so 1 ten is
  − 3 3 8     exchanged for 10 ones. 10 + 5 = 15
    3 0 7   ← 15 − 8 = 7
```
6 − 3 = 3   3 − 3 = 0

Set A

Find the answers by using one of the methods shown above:

1.
```
  8 7 3
− 6 2 1
```

2.
```
  5 4 7
− 3 3 5
```

3.
```
  9 6 5
− 4 4 3
```

4.
```
  4 8 9
− 2 5 7
```

5.
```
  6 8 2
− 3 5 1
```

6.
```
  7 3 8
− 5 2 6
```

7.
```
  9 4 7
− 7 2 8
```

8.
```
  5 8 4
− 2 6 6
```

9.
```
  4 9 7
− 2 5 9
```

Work out:

10. 729 − 108
11. 467 − 456
12. 386 − 152
13. 496 − 364
14. 592 − 375
15. 685 − 467

Set B

Find the answers:

1.
```
  7 8 6
− 2 5 4
```

2.
```
  4 8 7
− 3 7 5
```

3.
```
  5 7 2
− 3 5 5
```

4.
```
  7 8 3
− 2 5 7
```

5.
```
  9 5 8
− 4 6 1
```

6.
```
  8 3 9
− 5 4 5
```

Work out:

7. 384 − 253
8. 938 − 425
9. 747 − 539
10. 674 − 358
11. 708 − 562
12. 822 − 241

Find the number that is:

13. 425 less than 763
14. 508 less than 857
15. Fergus planted 784 seeds. Only 492 of them grew into plants. How many of the seeds didn't grow?

Set C

Find the answers:

1.
```
  6 8 6
− 3 5 8
```

2.
```
  7 4 3
− 4 7 9
```

3.
```
  5 0 4
− 3 7 5
```

Work out:

4. 305 − 194
5. 848 − 367
6. 683 − 255
7. 924 − 416
8. 565 − 382
9. 757 − 438

Anish made 128 brownies and 334 cupcakes.

10. How many more cupcakes than brownies did he make?

11. He sold 182 of the cupcakes. How many did he have left?

Phoebe has a stamp book with 867 spaces. She fills 575 spaces with stamps.

12. How many spaces does she have left?

13. Jaya has 784 stamps. How many more stamps does she have than Phoebe?

I can do written subtraction with 3-digit numbers.

  ✓   ✓   ✓

Now give some of these trickier subtractions a go.

Examples

A cat shelter has 184 cats. 49 of the cats are ginger. How many of the cats are not ginger?

$$
\begin{array}{r}
1\ \overset{7}{\cancel{8}}\ {}^{1}4 \\
-\quad 4\ 9 \\
\hline
1\ 3\ 5 \\
\end{array}
$$

Oliver owns a bakery. Every day he bakes 903 pies. 364 of them are vegetarian. How many are not vegetarian?

$$
\begin{array}{r}
\overset{8}{\cancel{9}}\ \overset{9}{\cancel{\cancel{0}}}\ {}^{1}3 \\
-\ 3\ 6\ 4 \\
\hline
5\ 3\ 9 \\
\end{array}
$$

You can't exchange any tens, so you need to exchange 1 hundred for 10 tens first.

Set A

Work out the answers:

1.
```
  299
-  38
```

2.
```
  275
-  54
```

3.
```
  452
-  43
```

4.
```
  761
-  45
```

5.
```
  634
-  43
```

6.
```
  842
-  61
```

Work out:

7. 158 – 27
8. 264 – 53
9. 894 – 56
10. 495 – 66
11. 634 – 72
12. 548 – 74

The table shows the numbers of stuffed animals in a toy shop.

Tiger	Elephant	Giraffe
376	83	68

13. How many more tigers than giraffes are there?

14. How many fewer elephants than tigers are there?

Set B

Work out the answers:

1.
```
  503
-  52
```

2.
```
  478
-  83
```

3.
```
  693
-  68
```

4.
```
  802
-  57
```

5.
```
  153
-  76
```

6.
```
  423
-  48
```

Work out:

7. 745 – 82
8. 483 – 96
9. 627 – 39
10. 847 – 26
11. 941 – 583
12. 527 – 265

Sara counted 736 stars on Monday, 218 on Tuesday and 547 on Wednesday.

13. How many fewer stars did she count on Tuesday than on Monday?

14. How many more stars did she count on Monday than on Wednesday?

Set C

Work out:

1.
```
  937
-  68
```

2.
```
  636
- 257
```

3.
```
  503
- 298
```

Work out:

4. 873 – 85
5. 907 – 78
6. 433 – 284
7. 654 – 497
8. 904 – 658
9. 506 – 367

607 trolls and 89 dragons invaded a castle with 358 knights inside.

10. How many more trolls were there than dragons?

11. How many fewer knights were there than trolls?

The table shows how far three children walk to school.

Jack	Molly	Lena
373 m	98 m	502 m

12. How much further does Jack walk than Molly?

13. How much further does Lena walk than Jack?

I am confident doing subtraction using written methods.

Addition and Subtraction — Review 4

Work out:

1 96
     − 3 4

2 68
     − 4 7

3 87
     − 6 2

4 42
     − 3 4

5 76
     − 5 9

6 44
     − 2 9

Work out these answers using a written method:

7 87 − 42

8 59 − 27

9 68 − 25

10 58 − 36

11 97 − 64

12 51 − 38

13 94 − 66

14 72 − 56

15 86 − 39

16 72 − 65

Work out these answers:

17 72 less than 93

18 37 less than 58

19 54 less than 73

20 28 less than 64

21 18 less than 66

22 54 less than 82

Work out:

23 857
      − 3 1 5

24 684
      − 2 5 3

25 536
      − 2 1 8

26 429
      − 2 5 3

27 752
      − 4 3 6

28 946
      − 3 6 2

Work out these answers using a written method:

29 483 − 261

30 784 − 453

31 597 − 385

32 948 − 329

33 836 − 353

34 645 − 173

35 934 − 426

36 326 − 255

Work out these answers:

37 364 less than 785

38 251 less than 694

39 238 less than 664

Kerry owns an ice cream van. She starts the day with 737 chocolate swirls and 849 vanilla pops.

40 She has 452 chocolate swirls left at the end of the day. How many did she sell?

41 She sold 583 vanilla pops. How many does she have left?

Work out:

42 584
      − 5 7

43 952
      − 8 1

44 604
      − 3 5

45 828
      − 3 4 9

46 715
      − 5 4 7

47 305
      − 1 7 6

Work out these answers using a written method:

48 268 − 45

49 494 − 76

50 527 − 81

51 652 − 77

52 834 − 56

53 732 − 339

54 574 − 385

55 225 − 186

56 921 − 374

57 502 − 267

58 Ainara guessed there were 613 jelly beans in a jar. The jar actually had 65 fewer jelly beans than she guessed. How many jelly beans were inside the jar?

The table shows how far Chris threw three paper aeroplanes.

Plane A	Plane B	Plane C
96 cm	703 cm	235 cm

How much further did Chris throw:

59 Plane B than Plane A?

60 Plane B than Plane C?

Phew, what a lot of questions! Well done for finishing them all!

Estimating

Estimating is a really useful way to get a rough idea of the answer.
It means you don't have to spend a lot of time working out the exact answer.

Examples

Write a simple calculation to estimate the answer to:

58 + 91

58 is close to 60   91 is close to 90

60 + 90

403 + 98

403 is close to 400   98 is close to 100

400 + 100

Set A

Write a calculation you could use to estimate these additions:

1. 61 + 38
2. 42 + 87
3. 79 + 49
4. 59 + 23
5. 398 + 11
6. 502 + 58

Write a calculation you could use to estimate these subtractions:

7. 81 – 58
8. 92 – 61
9. 78 – 69
10. 77 – 28
11. 401 – 18
12. 699 – 28

Choose the best estimate for the following calculations:

13. 38 + 71: 90 or 110
14. 12 + 61: 70 or 90
15. 93 – 21: 50 or 70
16. 298 + 49: 320 or 350
17. 452 – 29: 400 or 420
18. 681 – 59: 620 or 650

Set B

Write a calculation you could use to estimate these calculations:

1. 152 + 41
2. 519 + 82
3. 498 + 28
4. 781 – 62
5. 852 – 43
6. 448 – 132

Choose the best estimate for the following calculations:

7. 126 + 43: 170 or 200
8. 284 – 62: 190 or 220
9. 719 + 32: 720 or 750
10. 458 – 41: 390 or 420
11. 252 + 129: 350 or 380
12. 563 – 208: 350 or 400

Two of the calculations below are incorrect.

A: 263 + 79 = 342
B: 847 + 68 = 955
C: 981 – 38 = 913
D: 348 – 57 = 291

13. Use estimating to decide which two are incorrect.

Set C

Write a calculation you could use to estimate these calculations:

1. 321 + 62
2. 598 – 82
3. 289 – 172
4. 622 + 272
5. 297 + 631
6. 838 – 203

Choose the best estimate for the following calculations:

7. 308 + 294: 500 or 600
8. 492 + 298: 700 or 800
9. 731 + 172: 900 or 950
10. 953 – 382: 540 or 570
11. 692 – 531: 130 or 160
12. 541 + 458: 950 or 1000

Estimate then work out the answer to these calculations.

13. 847 + 38
14. 349 + 243
15. 328 + 557
16. 829 – 133
17. 922 – 719
18. 632 – 297

I can estimate answers to calculations.

Checking Calculations

Inverse operations can help you to check an answer to a calculation.
Inverse just means opposite — if you used + in the question, use − to check your answer.

Examples

Anita works out that 84 + 76 = 160. Write down an inverse calculation she could use to check her answer.

Write down an inverse calculation to check 534 − 82 = 452.

$$160 - 76 = \mathbf{84}$$
$$\text{OR } 160 - 84 = \mathbf{76}$$

$$452 + 82 = \mathbf{534}$$

Set A

Write down the answer to these inverse calculations:

1. 34 + 32 = 66.
   What is 66 − 34?
   What is 66 − 32?

2. 28 + 73 = 101.
   What is 101 − 73?

3. 98 − 23 = 75.
   What is 75 + 23?

For each of these, write an inverse calculation using the boxes to help.

4. 28 + 93 = 121 ⟶ ☐ − ☐ = ☐
5. 85 + 37 = 122 ⟶ ☐ − ☐ = ☐
6. 274 + 83 = 357 ⟶ ☐ − ☐ = ☐
7. 94 − 78 = 16 ⟶ ☐ + ☐ = ☐
8. 83 − 52 = 31 ⟶ ☐ + ☐ = ☐
9. 907 − 73 = 834 ⟶ ☐ + ☐ = ☐

Write an inverse calculation to check:

10. 42 + 84 = 126
11. 83 − 51 = 32
12. 64 − 36 = 28
13. 948 + 25 = 973
14. 326 + 37 = 363
15. 754 − 26 = 728

Set B

Write down the answer to these inverse calculations:

1. 837 + 78 = 915
   What is 915 − 78?

2. 926 + 42 = 968
   What is 968 − 42?
   What is 968 − 926?

3. 639 − 28 = 611.
   What is 611 + 28?

For each of these, write an inverse calculation using the boxes to help.

4. 298 + 78 = 376 ⟶ ☐ − ☐ = ☐
5. 955 + 35 = 990 ⟶ ☐ − ☐ = ☐
6. 654 + 218 = 872 ⟶ ☐ − ☐ = ☐
7. 649 − 42 = 607 ⟶ ☐ + ☐ = ☐
8. 503 − 267 = 236 ⟶ ☐ + ☐ = ☐
9. 684 − 506 = 178 ⟶ ☐ + ☐ = ☐

Two of the calculations below are incorrect.

A: 873 + 64 = 987
B: 732 + 241 = 973
C: 302 − 65 = 237
D: 936 − 423 = 573

10. Use inverse operations to check which two are incorrect.

Set C

Write an inverse calculation you could use to check:

1. 456 + 513 = 969
2. 395 + 287 = 682
3. 561 + 327 = 888
4. 739 − 537 = 202
5. 843 − 124 = 719
6. 957 − 254 = 703

Use inverse operations to check if these calculations are right or wrong:

7. 293 + 586 = 879
8. 374 + 406 = 740
9. 586 + 248 = 884
10. 976 − 564 = 412
11. 858 − 534 = 304
12. 453 − 211 = 242

Work out, then check with an inverse calculation:

13. 632 + 327
14. 384 + 423
15. 178 + 736
16. 692 − 342
17. 597 − 203
18. 643 − 421

I can check calculations using inverses.

These pages are full of lots more mental addition and subtraction practice.
Remember to read the question carefully before you decide which calculations you need to do.

Examples

An ice lolly costs 99p. Harvey has 64p.
How much more money does he need to buy the ice lolly?

$$99 - 64$$
$$= 99 - 60 - 4$$
$$= 39 - 4 = 35. \text{ So Harvey needs } \textbf{35p} \text{ more.}$$

Yusra invited all 82 people in her year to her birthday party.
59 of them came to the party. How many didn't come to the party?

$$82 - 59$$
$$= 82 - 60 + 1$$
$$= 22 + 1 = 23. \text{ So } \textbf{23 people} \text{ didn't come.}$$

Darcy ran 395 m. Luca ran 300 m further. How far did Luca run?

$$395 + 300$$
$$395 + 300 = 695. \text{ So Luca ran } \textbf{695 m.}$$
$$(3 + 3 = 6)$$

← Remember to write the units down once you have worked out the answer.

Set A

Georgia wants to buy these three things from a shop, but she only has £28.

£12   £19   £4

1   How much more money does she need?

2   She decides to buy the top and the belt. How much money will she have left?

Ellen took part in a quiz that had 60 questions.

3   She got 15 questions wrong. How many questions did she get right?

4   The winner got 52 questions right. How many of the questions did they get wrong?

5   A school ordered 250 maths textbooks and 40 science textbooks. How many textbooks did they order in total?

Fadila did 300 star jumps in the morning and 230 star jumps in the afternoon.

6   How many more star jumps did she do in the morning than in the afternoon?

7   How many star jumps did she do in total?

Oliver has a camera which can hold 550 pictures. He has taken 440 pictures.

8   How many more pictures can he take before the camera is full?

9   He deletes 30 of the pictures he has taken. How many pictures are left on the camera?

Thomas and Victoria collect monster cards. Thomas has 340 and Victoria has 460.

10   How many more monster cards does Victoria have than Thomas?

11   Thomas gives 30 cards to Victoria. How many cards do they each have now?

1. Nishant has 87p in his pocket.
   He wants to buy some sweets that cost 95p.
   How much more money does he need?

2. Ellis has 130 dance trophies and
   80 football trophies. How many
   trophies does he have altogether?

Rowley finished a puzzle in 150 seconds.
Chetna took 74 seconds longer than Rowley.

3. How long did it take Chetna to
   finish the puzzle?

4. How long did it take them in
   total to finish the puzzle?

Emily has 620 marbles.

5. 220 of her marbles are blue.
   How many are not blue?

6. Emily gives 140 of her marbles to Julia.
   How many marbles does Emily have left?

There are 180 snakes, 130 lizards and 75 tortoises
in the reptile house at the zoo.

7. How many more snakes
   are there than tortoises?

8. How many snakes, lizards and tortoises
   are there in total in the reptile house?

A local library is having a reading competition.
The first person to read 500 books wins a prize.
This table shows how many books three children
have read so far.

Charlie	Amelia	Neha
240	99	370

9. How many more books has Neha
   read than Charlie?

10. How many fewer books has Amelia
    read than Neha?

11. How many more books does Amelia
    need to read to win the prize?

Aviv counted 81 birds in his garden.

1. 49 of them were blackbirds.
   How many of the birds weren't blackbirds?

2. A cat came and scared 67 of the birds away.
   How many were left in the garden?

3. Sienna went to the park and
   counted 59 more birds than Aviv.
   How many birds did Sienna count?

The table shows how far Kai travels in
different events on sports day.

Hopping	57 m
Jumping	49 m
Skipping	205 m

4. How far does he travel in total?

5. Masie hops 19 m further than Kai hops.
   How far does she hop?

6. Alf hops and jumps the same distance as Kai
   but skips 37 m less. How far does he travel?

7. Ted took part in a 500 m race.
   He hurt his foot when he was 79 m
   from the finish line and had to stop.
   How far did Ted run?

A computer tablet costs £189
and a laptop costs £390.

8. How much more expensive
   is the laptop than the tablet?

9. How much would it cost to buy both
   the laptop and the tablet?

10. The price of the laptop is £65 cheaper in a
    sale. How much does the laptop cost now?

11. There are 844 apples in a shop.
    470 of them are red. How many are not red?

12. Pam needs to find 650 diamonds to
    unlock the next level of her game.
    She has found 423 diamonds so far.
    How many more does she need to find?

I can solve problems using mental addition and subtraction.

Addition and Subtraction Problems — 2

You'll need to use some of the written methods for these questions.
Just like before think carefully about what the question is asking you to do before you try to solve it.

Examples

Mariah's school is releasing balloons as part of a geography project.
There are 562 pupils at the school. The school has bought 938 balloons.

If every pupil has 1 balloon, how many extra balloons will there be?

938 − 562 =

$$
\begin{array}{r}
{}^8\cancel{9}\,{}^1 3\ 8 \\
-\ 5\ 6\ 2 \\
\hline
3\ 7\ 6
\end{array}
$$

So there will be **376 extra balloons**.

So far, 97 of the balloons have been blown up. How many are left to blow up?

938 − 97 =

$$
\begin{array}{r}
{}^8\cancel{9}\,{}^1 3\ 8 \\
-\quad 9\ 7 \\
\hline
8\ 4\ 1
\end{array}
$$

So **841 balloons** still need to be blown up.

There are 67 teachers at the school. How many teachers and pupils are there in total?

562 + 67 =

$$
\begin{array}{r}
5\ 6\ 2 \\
+\quad 6\ 7 \\
\hline
6\ 2\ 9 \\
{}_1
\end{array}
$$

So there are **629 teachers and pupils**.

Set A

There are 95 words on a spelling test. The table shows how many words each child spelt right.

Delia	35
Henry	43
Samson	58
Zane	19

1 How many words did Henry spell wrong?

2 How many more words did Samson spell right than Zane?

3 How many words did Henry and Delia spell right in total?

Teresa buys 26 blue stickers, 32 pink stickers and 31 orange stickers.

4 How many stickers does she have in total?

5 She gives out 86 of the stickers to her class. How many does she have left?

6 Kayla has 124 red pens and 235 blue pens. How many pens does she have in total?

Brad is thinking of a number.
He takes 56 away from it and gets 234.

7 Sophie says the Brad was thinking of 178 because 234 − 56 = 178. Can you explain where Sophie went wrong?

8 What was Brad's original number?

The table shows how long it took four children to solve a riddle.

Name	Time
Ed	311 seconds
Adva	422 seconds
Jed	718 seconds
Scarlett	521 seconds

9 What was the total time of Adva and Ed?

10 How much quicker was Ed than Scarlett?

11 How much slower was Jed than Adva?

12 There are 786 carrots in a field. A farmer picks 345 of them. How many carrots are left?

Set B

Pupils can choose between three different clubs after school on Tuesday. The table shows the number of pupils that go to each club.

Ballet	Drama	Tennis
45	83	68

1. How many more pupils go to drama than tennis?

2. How many pupils go to either ballet or tennis?

3. 17 children stop going to drama and start going to ballet instead. How many pupils now attend each club?

Ron has 563 gnomes in his garden.

4. Ron's brother has 371 gnomes in his garden. How many gnomes do they have in total?

5. 485 of Ron's gnomes have beards. How many do not have beards?

6. One night, a storm blows 82 of Ron's gnomes away. How many gnomes does Ron have left?

There are 876 houses and 118 shops in a village.

7. How many houses and shops are there in total?

8. 748 of the houses have chimneys. How many don't have chimneys?

9. Carlota is building a toy car. It weighs 638 g with the wheels and 497 g without the wheels. How much do the wheels weigh?

10. Rav has three rolls of ribbon. The first roll has 138 cm of ribbon, the second has 219 cm and the third has 342 cm. How much ribbon does Rav have in total?

11. Chloe is trying to work out the answer to 187 + 498. She estimates an answer by working out 190 + 500 = 690. How far away from the actual answer is her estimate?

Set C

There are two adult giraffes at the zoo. Geraldine has 183 spots and Marvin has 216.

1. How many fewer spots does Geraldine have than Marvin?

2. A third giraffe, Jerry, arrives at the zoo. In total, Jerry and Marvin have 404 spots. How many spots does Jerry have?

3. Geraldine has a baby which is born with 68 spots. How many more spots does Geraldine have than her baby?

There are 738 cars in a car park. 437 of them are blue.

4. How many of them are not blue?

5. 248 more cars arrive. How many cars are there in the car park in total?

6. Mia collects 286 shells from the beach, Archie collects 138 shells and Sally collects 84 shells. How many do they have in total?

Charlotte is selling raffle tickets at the school fair. The table shows how many she sold.

Red	Yellow	Blue
187	363	254

7. How many more yellow tickets did she sell than blue tickets?

8. How many red and blue tickets did she sell?

9. How many tickets did Charlotte sell in total?

There are 822 frog eggs in the school pond. The table shows how many turn into tadpoles each day.

Wednesday	Thursday	Friday
134	63	204

10. How many eggs were left in the pond after Wednesday?

11. How many eggs hatched on Thursday and Friday?

12. How many eggs were left after Friday?

I can solve problems using written addition and subtraction.

Addition and Subtraction — Review 5

Write a calculation you could use
to estimate these calculations.

1. 83 + 71
2. 98 + 53
3. 702 + 39
4. 582 + 71
5. 239 + 598
6. 621 + 198
7. 97 – 31
8. 68 – 29
9. 738 – 47
10. 851 – 72
11. 963 – 242
12. 739 – 597

Choose the best estimate for these calculations.

13. 99 + 52:   150   200   250
14. 74 + 19:   70   90   110
15. 86 – 38:   30   50   70
16. 878 – 99:   740   780   820
17. 528 + 63:   550   590   630
18. 159 + 727:   810   850   890
19. 537 – 204:   310   340   370

Use inverse calculations to answer these questions:

20. 73 + 58 = 131. What is 131 – 58?
21. 78 – 26 = 52. What is 52 + 26?
22. 494 + 87 = 581. What is 581 – 87?
23. 487 – 56 = 431. What is 431 + 56?
24. 648 – 327 = 321. What is 321 + 327?
25. 375 + 527 = 902. What is 902 – 375?

Write an inverse calculation using the boxes to help:

26. 89 + 36 = 125 ⟶ ☐ – ☐ = ☐
27. 739 + 36 = 775 ⟶ ☐ – ☐ = ☐
28. 173 + 681 = 854 ⟶ ☐ – ☐ = ☐
29. 96 – 35 = 61 ⟶ ☐ + ☐ = ☐
30. 351 – 28 = 323 ⟶ ☐ + ☐ = ☐
31. 934 – 526 = 408 ⟶ ☐ + ☐ = ☐

Write an inverse calculation you could use
to check the answers to these questions:

32. 47 + 56 = 103
33. 785 + 65 = 850
34. 675 + 265 = 940
35. 63 – 45 = 18
36. 374 – 68 = 306
37. 439 – 285 = 154

Work out the answers to these questions then
check your answers using an inverse calculation.

38. 68 + 65
39. 654 + 92
40. 375 + 284
41. 78 – 62
42. 194 – 74
43. 627 – 245

In a cycling shop, a bike costs £280
and a helmet costs £50.

44. What is the total cost of the bike and the helmet?

45. How much more does the bike cost
than the helmet?

A chef buys 160 mushrooms and 89 carrots.

46. How many mushrooms and carrots does
he buy in total?

47. He uses 72 of the mushrooms.
How many mushrooms does he have left?

Olivia has 506 fairy lights in her garden.

48. 212 of the lights don't work.
How many fairy lights do work?

49. Olivia bought another 86 fairy lights at the market.
How many fairy lights does she have in total?

Percy has made 354 ice cubes for a party.

50. Paco brings a bag of 257 ice cubes and
Gwen brings 142 ice cubes. How many
ice cubes do they have in total?

51. Before the party starts 67 of Percy's ice cubes melt.
How many does he have left?

Great work solving all those problems!

1 Look at this bar model:

790	
450	340

a) Write 2 additions and 2 subtractions using the three numbers in the bar model.

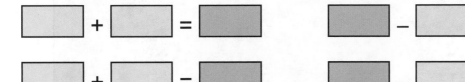

b) Write the correct numbers to complete these bar models:

450	
125	

120	
	490	190

240	270	180

c) Draw some of your own bar models but leave one bar blank.
   Give them to a friend and see if they can fill in the missing numbers on the bars.

2 Three children try to work out 678 + 98 in their head. They each explain their methods below.

I added on 100 then subtracted 2.

I added on 22 then added on 74.

I added on 2 then added on 100.

Elsa

Aya

Archie

a) Whose method do you think will give the right answer?

b) Can you explain what the other children have done wrong?

Rue is playing a space game. Each rock shows how many points she gains or loses for landing there.

a) Rue started the level with 150 points and then landed on all of the green rocks once each. How many points does Rue have now?

b) To get to the next level, Rue needs 450 points. Using her points from the last level, how many times does she have to land on the red rock to get enough points for the next level?

c) Rue's brother wants to play. He starts with 0 points and lands on 3 different rocks. What is the maximum number of points he could have?

d) If Rue's brother ends the level with 5 points, which 3 rocks could he have landed on? Can you find some other rocks he could have landed on?

4

The aim of the maze is to get from point A to point B without going back on yourself.
Pink stars are worth 35 points.
Blue stars are worth −30 points.
Green stars are worth 50 points.

a) Can you find a path through the maze that collects every star? How many points would you have at the end? Remember that you can't go back the same way you've come.

b) How many points would you have if you took the shortest possible route through the maze?

c) Draw your own maze with stars in and challenge your friends to find their way through it. See who can get through the maze with the most points.

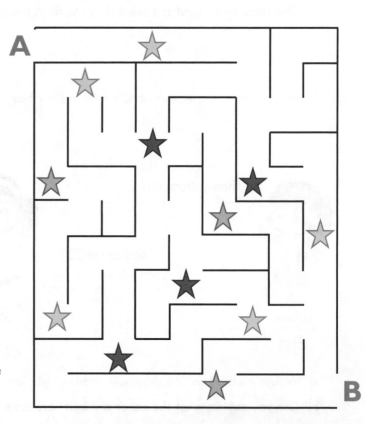

5

Rosanna is playing a game at the fair. She throws balls through the hoops to win points.

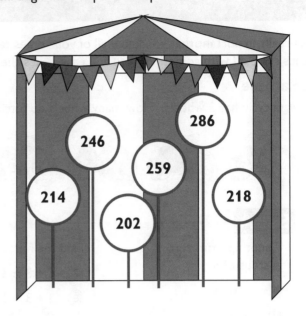

What is the maximum number of points she can get:

a) by throwing 2 balls through the same hoop?

b) by throwing 2 balls through different hoops?

c) by throwing 3 balls through different hoops?

d) Rosanna threw a ball through the hoop worth 286 points. She then threw another 2 balls through different hoops. Her total score was 734 points. Which 2 hoops did she throw the balls through?

---

7 pirates, a parrot and a monkey have been looting an island. They have found 128 kg of treasure. Their ship can only carry 500 kg. The table shows how much the pirates and animals weigh.

Pirate	Weight
Barbalarga	45 kg
Grubby McGubbins	65 kg
Redbeard	72 kg
Hallie Silver	61 kg
Ratty Bobkins	50 kg
Siren Delmar	60 kg
Captain Roger	95 kg
Molly the Monkey	3 kg
Paul the Parrot	2 kg

a) What is the total weight of all the pirates and animals?

b) If the pirates leave Redbeard, Molly the Monkey and Paul the Parrot behind on the island, can they take all of the treasure? Explain your answer.

c) Who is the lightest pirate they can leave behind if they:

i) want to take all of the treasure.

ii) leave half of the treasure behind.

These pages were pretty tough, but you've made it through. Well done!

The 3 Times Table

It's really important that you know all of your times tables.
Let's start off with something nice and easy — it's the 3s.

Example

A tricycle has 3 wheels. How many wheels do 5 tricycles have?

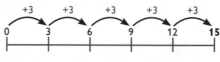

$$3 + 3 + 3 + 3 + 3 = 5 \times 3 = 15$$

Set A

Count up from zero
in steps of 3:

1. 2 steps
2. 6 steps
3. 7 steps
4. 8 steps
5. 10 steps
6. 12 steps

Find the missing values:

7. $3 + 3 + 3 = 3 \times 3 = \boxed{}$
8. $3 + 3 + 3 + 3 + 3 + 3 + 3$
   $= \boxed{} \times 3 = \boxed{}$
9. $\boxed{} \times 3 = 3$
10. $4 \times 3 = \boxed{}$
11. $9 \times 3 = \boxed{}$
12. $\boxed{} \times 3 = 33$

Answer the following:

13. 5×3
14. 6×3
15. 12×3

Are the following true or false?

16. $6 \times 3 = 8 + 8$
17. $8 \times 3 = 12 \times 2$

Set B

Answer the following:

1. 1×3
2. 4×3
3. 7×3
4. 8×3
5. 0×3
6. 11×3
7. 12×3

Which symbol (<, > or =)
should go in each box?

8. $3 \times 3 \boxed{} 9$
9. $5 \times 3 \boxed{} 17$
10. $28 \boxed{} 9 \times 3$
11. $3 \times 2 \boxed{} 2 \times 3$
12. $3 + 3 \boxed{} 3 \times 3$
13. $6 \times 3 \boxed{} 3 + 9 + 3$

What are:

14. eight lots of three?
15. eleven lots of three?

A triangle has three sides.
How many sides are there on:

16. three triangles?
17. ten triangles?
18. twelve triangles?

Set C

Find the missing values:

1. $5 \times 3 = \boxed{}$
2. $8 \times 3 = \boxed{}$
3. $\boxed{} \times 3 = 30$
4. $\boxed{} \times 3 = 10 + 2$
5. $2 \times 3 = \boxed{} \times 1$
6. $9 \times 3 = 20 + \boxed{}$
7. $12 \times 3 = \boxed{} \times 2$

Are these numbers in
the 3 times table?

8. twenty-eight
9. eighteen

There are 3 tennis balls in a can.
How many tennis balls are there in:

10. three cans?
11. seven cans?
12. ten cans?

Stools and tripods each have 3 legs.
How many legs will there be on:

13. four stools?
14. six tripods?
15. one tripod and one stool?
16. five tripods and four stools?
17. eight stools and four tripods?
18. eleven stools and no tripods?

I know and can use the 3 times table.

The 4 Times Table

Now it's time to tackle the 4 times table.
Make sure you're happy counting up in steps of four before tackling this page.

Example

A lucky clover has 4 leaves. How many leaves do 6 lucky clovers have?

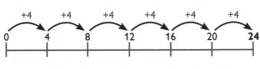

$$4 + 4 + 4 + 4 + 4 + 4 = 6 \times 4 = 24$$

Set A

Count up from zero in steps of 4:

1. 1 step
2. 3 steps
3. 6 steps
4. 7 steps
5. 9 steps
6. 11 steps

Find the missing values:

7. $4 + 4 = 2 \times 4 = \boxed{}$
8. $4 + 4 + 4 + 4 + 4 = \boxed{} \times 4 = \boxed{}$
9. $\boxed{} \times 4 = 0$
10. $4 \times 4 = \boxed{}$
11. $8 \times 4 = \boxed{}$
12. $\boxed{} \times 4 = 36$

Answer the following:

13. 10×4
14. 6×4
15. 12×4

Are the following true or false?

16. 30 is in the 4 times table.
17. $5 \times 4 = 10 \times 2$

Set B

Answer the following:

1. 3×4
2. 0×4
3. 5×4
4. 6×4
5. 8×4
6. 11×4
7. 12×4

8. Which numbers in the box below are in the 4 times table?

8	10	14	20
26	32	38	42

Which symbol (<, > or =) should go in each box?

9. $9 \times 4 \boxed{} 32$
10. $4 \times 7 \boxed{} 7 \times 4$
11. $4 + 4 + 4 \boxed{} 4 \times 4$

There are 4 people on a bobsleigh team. How many people are on:

12. two bobsleigh teams?
13. seven bobsleigh teams?
14. ten bobsleigh teams?

There are 4 seasons in a year. How many seasons are there in:

15. eight years?
16. twelve years?

Set C

Find the missing values:

1. $5 \times 4 = \boxed{}$
2. $7 \times 4 = \boxed{}$
3. $\boxed{} \times 4 = 40$
4. $4 \times 4 = 10 + \boxed{}$
5. $0 \times 4 = \boxed{}$
6. $11 \times 4 = 40 + \boxed{}$
7. $8 \times 4 = \boxed{} \times 2$

Cows have 4 legs. How many legs do:

8. six cows have?
9. nine cows have?

Are the following true or false?

10. All the numbers in the 4 times table are even.
11. All even numbers are in the 4 times table.

Squares and rectangles each have 4 sides. How many sides do:

12. ten squares have?
13. one square and three rectangles have?
14. six squares and five rectangles have?
15. nine squares and seven rectangles have?

I know and can use the 4 times table.

The 8 Times Table

The final times table that you need to learn in Year 3 is the 8s.

Examples

An octopus has 8 tentacles.
How many tentacles do 4 octopuses have?

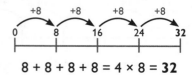

$8 + 8 + 8 + 8 = 4 \times 8 = \mathbf{32}$

Is 76 in the 8 times table?

$9 \times 8 = 72$ and $10 \times 8 = 80$

No, 76 is not in the 8 times table.

Set A

Count up from zero in steps of 8:

1. 2 steps
2. 4 steps
3. 6 steps
4. 7 steps
5. 9 steps
6. 12 steps

Find the missing values:

7. $8 + 8 + 8 = 3 \times 8 = \boxed{}$
8. $8 + 8 + 8 + 8 + 8 = \boxed{} \times 8 = \boxed{}$
9. $\boxed{} \times 8 = 8$
10. $4 \times 8 = \boxed{}$
11. $10 \times 8 = \boxed{}$
12. $\boxed{} \times 8 = 88$

Answer the following:

13. 6×8
14. 8×8
15. 12×8

Which symbol (<, > or =) should go in each box?

16. $8 \times 5 \boxed{} 4 \times 8$
17. $9 \times 8 \boxed{} 70 + 8$

Set B

Answer the following:

1. 1×8
2. 4×8
3. 6×8
4. 0×8
5. 7×8
6. 10×8
7. 11×8

Are the following true or false?

8. $8 \times 3 = 8 + 8 + 8$
9. $9 \times 8 = 80 + 8$
10. $12 \times 8 = 100 - 4$
11. Which numbers below are **not** in the 8 times table?

8	12	18	24
40	56	60	64

What are:

12. two lots of eight?
13. eleven lots of eight?

There are 8 sausages in a pack. How many sausages are in:

14. five packs?
15. eight packs?
16. twelve packs?

Set C

Find the missing values:

1. $2 \times 8 = \boxed{}$
2. $8 \times 8 = \boxed{}$
3. $\boxed{} \times 8 = 80$
4. $8 \times \boxed{} = 0$
5. $5 \times 8 = \boxed{} \times 10$
6. $8 \times 8 = 60 + \boxed{}$
7. $3 \times 8 = \boxed{} \times 2$

One bottle of orange juice can fill 8 glasses. How many glasses can:

8. five bottles fill?
9. nine bottles fill?
10. eleven bottles fill?
11. Is this sentence true or false?

"There are no numbers that are in both the 8 times table and the 5 times table."

Spiders and scorpions both have 8 legs. How many legs do:

12. nine spiders have?
13. three spiders and two scorpions have?
14. five spiders and seven scorpions have?
15. ten spiders and ten scorpions have?

I know and can use the 8 times table.

Division Facts

The opposite of multiplication is division. If you know your times tables, you can write down the answer to simple division questions too.

Examples

Caleb is sharing 24 cupcakes equally between his friends.
How many cupcakes does each person get if he shares them between:

3 friends?

$8 \times 3 = 24$
So $24 \div 3 =$ **8 cupcakes**

4 friends?

$6 \times 4 = 24$
So $24 \div 4 =$ **6 cupcakes**

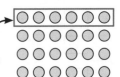

Set A

Find the missing values:

1. $3 \times 4 = 12$
   so $12 \div 4 = \boxed{3}$

2. $5 \times 8 = 40$
   so $40 \div 8 = \boxed{5}$

3. $9 \times 8 = 72$
   so $72 \div 8 = \boxed{9}$

4. $12 \times 3 = 36$
   so $36 \div 3 = \boxed{12}$

Answer the following:

5. $15 \div 3 = 5$

6. $21 \div 3 = 7$

7. $16 \div 4 = 4$

8. $32 \div 4$

9. $30 \div 3$

10. $48 \div 8$

11. $88 \div 8$

Which symbol (<, > or =) should go in each box?

12. $8 \div 4 \boxed{=} 2$

13. $20 \div 4 \boxed{<} 6$

14. $56 \div 8 \boxed{>} 6$

15. $33 \div 3 \boxed{=} 11$

16. $40 \div 4 \boxed{=} 10$

17. $96 \div 8 \boxed{>} 11$

Set B

Answer the following:

1. $28 \div 4$

2. $40 \div 8$

3. $33 \div 3$

4. $64 \div 8$

5. $48 \div 4$

6. $27 \div 3$

Which symbol (<, > or =) should go in each box?

7. $18 \div 2 \boxed{} 36 \div 4$

8. $32 \div 8 \boxed{} 12 \div 4$

9. $25 \div 5 \boxed{} 56 \div 8$

10. Which of the divisions below give the same answer?

   | $30 \div 5$ | $40 \div 8$ | $24 \div 4$ |

How many stickers will be in each pile if:

11. 44 stickers are divided into 4 equal piles?

12. 30 stickers are divided into 3 equal piles?

13. 72 stickers are divided into 8 equal piles?

Set C

Find the missing values:

1. $\boxed{} \div 1 = 8$

2. $\boxed{} \div 8 = 6$

3. $\boxed{} \div 3 = 9$

4. $32 \div \boxed{} = 4$

5. $24 \div \boxed{} = 6$

6. $44 \div \boxed{} = 11$

7. $96 \div \boxed{} = 12$

How many animals are in each pen if:

8. 24 donkeys are split equally between 3 pens? $= 8$

9. 36 cows are split equally between 4 pens? $= 9$

10. 88 sheep are split equally between 8 pens? $= 11$

11. 20 sheep and 8 cows are split equally between 4 pens? $= 7$

Football trading cards come in packs of 8. How many cards will each person get if:

12. 4 packs are shared equally between 2 people? $= 4$

13. 5 packs are shared equally between 10 people? $= 50$

14. 6 packs are shared equally between 4 people? $= 24$

I can use division facts from times tables.

Multiplication and Division — Review 1

Find the missing values:

1   3 + 3 + 3 + 3
    = ☐ × 3 = ☐

2   3 + 3 + 3 + 3 + 3
    = ☐ × 3 = ☐

3   2 × 3 = ☐

4   7 × 3 = ☐

5   1 × ☐ = 3

6   ☐ × 3 = 18

7   11 × 3 = ☐

8   ☐ × 3 = 12

9   3 × ☐ = 30

10 ☐ × 3 = 36

11 3 × 3 = ☐ × 9

12 3 × ☐ = 20 + 4

13 9 × 3 = 3 × ☐

Find the missing values:

33 8 + 8 + 8
    = ☐ × 8 = ☐

34 8 + 8 + 8 + 8
    = ☐ × 8 = ☐

35 ☐ × 8 = 64

36 7 × 8 = ☐

37 1 × ☐ = 8

38 ☐ × 8 = 40

39 11 × 8 = ☐

40 ☐ × 8 = 16

41 10 × ☐ = 80

42 ☐ × 8 = 96

43 3 × 8 = ☐ + 5

44 8 × ☐ = 50 − 2

45 9 × 8 = 8 × ☐

Are the following true or false?

14 21 is in the
    3 times table.

15 32 is in the
    3 times table.

16 8 × 3 < 3 × 6

17 6 × 3 = 12 × 2

18 9 × 3 > 5 × 5

There are 8 rowers on a rowing team.
How many rowers will there be on:

46 seven rowing teams?

47 nine rowing teams?

48 twelve rowing teams?

Jenny has £2 in her pocket.
Anders has 3 times as much money as Jenny.
Hassan has 3 times as much money as Anders.

19 How much money does Anders have?

20 How much money does Hassan have?

Are the following true or false?

49 All the numbers in the 8 times table are even.

50 All the numbers in the 8 times table
    are also in the 3 times table.

Answer the following:

21 0 × 4

22 1 × 4

23 4 × 4

24 7 × 4

25 9 × 4

26 12 × 4

Answer the following:

51 8 ÷ 4

52 32 ÷ 8

53 44 ÷ 4

54 18 ÷ 3

55 20 ÷ 4

56 24 ÷ 3

57 36 ÷ 4

58 33 ÷ 3

59 56 ÷ 8

60 72 ÷ 8

61 36 ÷ 3

62 48 ÷ 4

Look at the numbers in the box below:

6	10	14	18	20
31	34	36	37	44

27 Which numbers are in the 3 times table?

28 Which numbers are in the 4 times table?

Cartons of juice come in packs of 8.
How many packs do you need to buy to get:

63 64 cartons?

64 96 cartons?

Which symbol (<, > or =) should go in each box?

29 8 × 4 ☐ 22

30 10 × 4 ☐ 30 + 10

31 8 × 2 ☐ 6 × 4

32 9 × 4 ☐ 36 × 1

Tulip bulbs are sold in packs of 4.
How many bulbs will be in each pot if:

65 9 packs are split between 3 pots?

66 12 packs are split between 8 pots?

Congrats on getting through all those questions — you must be a times table whizz!

Mental Multiplication

Knowing your times tables can help you multiply even bigger numbers in your head.
Here you'll multiply multiples of 10 using your 2, 3, 4, 5 and 8 times tables.

Examples

Work out 20 × 3.

$2 × 3 = 6$
So $20 × 3 =$ **60**

Doughnuts come in boxes of 4.
How many doughnuts would there be in 80 boxes?

$8 × 4 = 32$
So $80 × 4 =$ **320 doughnuts**

Set A

Find the missing values:

1. $6 × 2 = 12$
   $60 × 2 = \boxed{}$
2. $5 × 3 = 15$
   $50 × 3 = \boxed{}$
3. $6 × 4 = 24$
   $60 × 4 = \boxed{}$
4. $7 × 3 = 21$
   $70 × 3 = \boxed{}$

Work out the missing values:

5. $6 × 5 = \boxed{}$
   $60 × 5 = \boxed{}$
6. $7 × 4 = \boxed{}$
   $70 × 4 = \boxed{}$
7. $3 × 8 = \boxed{}$
   $30 × 8 = \boxed{}$
   $3 × 80 = \boxed{}$

Use your times tables to work out:

8. $30 × 2$
9. $50 × 5$
10. $60 × 3$
11. $70 × 2$
12. $90 × 4$
13. $40 × 8$
14. $70 × 8$

Set B

Find the missing values:

1. $7 × 5 = \boxed{}$
   $70 × 5 = \boxed{}$
2. $6 × 4 = \boxed{}$
   $60 × 4 = \boxed{}$
3. $4 × 8 = \boxed{}$
   $40 × 8 = \boxed{}$
   $4 × 80 = \boxed{}$

Use your times tables to work out:

4. $40 × 2$
5. $90 × 5$
6. $30 × 4$
7. $50 × 8$
8. $120 × 3$
9. $110 × 8$

A slice of bread weighs 30 grams.
What is the total weight of:

10. 5 slices?
11. 8 slices?
12. Which of the calculations in the box below are correct?

> A: $2 × 5 × 4 = 2 × 20$
> B: $2 × 5 × 4 = 10 × 20$
> C: $2 × 5 × 4 = 10 × 4$

Set C

Work out:

1. $80 × 2$
2. $70 × 5$
3. $90 × 3$
4. $100 × 4$
5. $110 × 3$
6. $120 × 8$

Find the missing values:

7. $\boxed{} × 4 = 360$
8. $\boxed{} × 8 = 480$

A bottle of perfume contains 70 ml. How much will:

9. 4 bottles contain?
10. 8 bottles contain?

How much money (in pence) do you have if you have:

11. four 20p and nine 50p coins?
12. eleven 20p and two 50p coins?

Find the missing values:

13. $3 × 6 × 5 = 3 × \boxed{} = \boxed{}$
14. $8 × 4 × 5 = 8 × \boxed{} = \boxed{}$

I can use times tables to multiply bigger numbers.

Mental Division

Keep brushing up on those times tables — you'll need them again to tackle this page.
It's all about dividing multiples of 10 using the times table facts that you know.

Example

Daniel has a jar with 320 buttons in it. He shares the buttons equally between 4 tubs.
How many buttons will be in each tub?

$32 \div 4 = 8$
So $320 \div 4 = \mathbf{80}$

There will be **80 buttons** in each tub.

Set A

Find the missing values:

1. $8 \div 2 = 4$
   $80 \div 2 = \boxed{}$

2. $9 \div 3 = 3$
   $90 \div 3 = \boxed{}$

3. $12 \div 3 = 4$
   $120 \div 3 = \boxed{}$

4. $24 \div 4 = 6$
   $240 \div 4 = \boxed{}$

Work out the missing values:

5. $16 \div 8 = \boxed{}$
   $160 \div 8 = \boxed{}$

6. $45 \div 5 = \boxed{}$
   $450 \div 5 = \boxed{}$

7. $32 \div 4 = \boxed{}$
   $320 \div 4 = \boxed{}$

8. $30 \div 5 = \boxed{}$
   $300 \div 5 = \boxed{}$

Work out:

9. $60 \div 3$

10. $150 \div 5$

11. $180 \div 2$

12. $250 \div 5$

13. $240 \div 8$

14. $300 \div 3$

15. $400 \div 8$

Set B

Find the missing values:

1. $15 \div 3 = 5$
   $150 \div 3 = \boxed{}$

2. $16 \div 4 = 4$
   $160 \div 4 = \boxed{}$

3. $55 \div 5 = \boxed{}$
   $550 \div 5 = \boxed{}$

4. $32 \div 8 = \boxed{}$
   $320 \div 8 = \boxed{}$

Work out:

5. $40 \div 2$

6. $250 \div 5$

7. $280 \div 4$

8. $480 \div 8$

9. $330 \div 3$

10. $360 \div 4$

11. $720 \div 8$

There are 240 pupils at sports day. How many teams will there be if there are:

12. 3 pupils on each team?

13. 4 pupils on each team?

14. 8 pupils on each team?

15. A vine of 600 grapes is split into five equal bunches. How many grapes are in each bunch?

Set C

Work out:

1. $180 \div 2$

2. $350 \div 5$

3. $270 \div 3$

4. $440 \div 4$

5. $360 \div 3$

6. $800 \div 8$

Are the following true or false?

7. $120 \div 3 = 80 \div 2$

8. $550 \div 5 = 900 \div 10$

9. $560 \div 8 = 210 \div 3$

10. A whole cheesecake weighs 360 g and is cut into four equal slices. How much does each slice weigh?

Class 3A raised £480 for charity. How much will each charity get if they share it equally between:

11. 4 charities?

12. 8 charities?

13. Jo shares 960 ml of pineapple squash equally between 8 jugs. How many ml are in each jug?

I can use times tables to divide bigger numbers.

Division using Chunking

You can make tricky divisions a bit simpler by chunking them up. Start with the number you're dividing and subtract multiples of the number you're dividing by until you get to 0.

Example

Work out 42 ÷ 3.

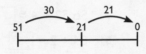

There are 10 + 4 = 14 threes in 42.
So 42 ÷ 3 = **14**.

You can also start at 0 and add up in chunks until you get to the number you're dividing.

Set A

Use the number lines to work out:

1. 52 ÷ 4
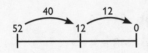

2. 70 ÷ 5
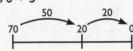

3. 51 ÷ 3
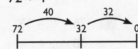

4. 72 ÷ 4

Work out:

5. 39 ÷ 3
6. 34 ÷ 2
7. 65 ÷ 5
8. 60 ÷ 4
9. 48 ÷ 3
10. 68 ÷ 4
11. 57 ÷ 3

Set B

Use the number lines to work out:

1. 80 ÷ 5
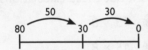

2. 56 ÷ 4
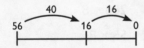

Work out these divisions:

3. 38 ÷ 2
4. 42 ÷ 3
5. 85 ÷ 5
6. 64 ÷ 4
7. 45 ÷ 3
8. 54 ÷ 3
9. 76 ÷ 4

Work out:

10. 72 ÷ 3
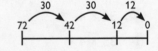

11. 84 ÷ 4
12. 115 ÷ 5
13. 78 ÷ 3

Set C

Use the number lines to work out:

1. 96 ÷ 4
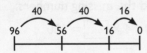

2. 75 ÷ 3
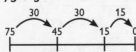

Work out these divisions:

3. 54 ÷ 3
4. 75 ÷ 5
5. 68 ÷ 4
6. 95 ÷ 5
7. 69 ÷ 3
8. 81 ÷ 3
9. 92 ÷ 4

Work out:

10. 74 ÷ 2
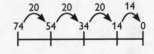

11. 165 ÷ 5
12. 102 ÷ 3
13. 140 ÷ 4

I can use chunking to divide numbers.

Doubling and Halving

You can use repeated doubling and halving to multiply and divide by 4 or 8 in your head.

Examples

Work out 25 × 4 by doubling 25 two times.

25 × 2 = 50
50 × 2 = 100
So 25 × 4 = **100**

Multiplying by 4 is the same as doubling twice.

Work out 120 ÷ 8 by halving 120 three times.

120 ÷ 2 = 60
60 ÷ 2 = 30
30 ÷ 2 = 15
So 120 ÷ 8 = **15**

Dividing by 8 is the same as halving three times.

Set A

Find the missing numbers:

1. 14 × 2 = 28
   28 × 2 = 56
   So 14 × 4 = ☐

2. 22 × 2 = 44
   44 × 2 = ☐
   So 22 × 4 = ☐

3. 45 × 2 = ☐
   ☐ × 2 = ☐
   So 45 × 4 = ☐

Find the missing numbers:

4. 52 ÷ 2 = 26
   26 ÷ 2 = 13
   So 52 ÷ 4 = ☐

5. 84 ÷ 2 = ☐
   ☐ ÷ 2 = ☐
   So 84 ÷ 4 = ☐

6. 76 ÷ 2 = 38
   38 ÷ 2 = ☐
   So 76 ÷ 4 = ☐

Double or halve two times to work out these calculations:

7. 15 × 4
8. 64 ÷ 4
9. 48 ÷ 4
10. 23 × 4
11. 40 × 4
12. 88 ÷ 4
13. 120 ÷ 4

Set B

Double and double again to work out these multiplications:

1. 30 × 4
2. 35 × 4
3. 45 × 4
4. 31 × 4
5. 42 × 4
6. 17 × 4

Halve and halve again to work out these divisions:

7. 100 ÷ 4
8. 84 ÷ 4
9. 92 ÷ 4
10. 128 ÷ 4
11. 300 ÷ 4
12. 148 ÷ 4

Double or halve three times to work out these calculations:

13. 13 × 8
14. 15 × 8
15. 160 ÷ 8
16. 200 ÷ 8
17. 55 × 8
18. 600 ÷ 8

Set C

Use doubling to work out:

1. 18 × 4
2. 35 × 8
3. 65 × 4
4. 51 × 4
5. 22 × 8
6. 31 × 8

Use halving to work out:

7. 96 ÷ 4
8. 280 ÷ 4
9. 400 ÷ 8
10. 360 ÷ 8
11. 164 ÷ 4
12. 1000 ÷ 8

Use doubling and halving to find the missing numbers:

13. 4 × ☐ = 200
14. ☐ ÷ 4 = 27
15. ☐ × 8 = 440
16. ☐ ÷ 8 = 65
17. 8 × ☐ = 680

I can mentally multiply and divide using doubling and halving.

Multiplication and Division — Review 2

Find the missing values in these multiplications:

1 9 × 3 = 27
90 × 3 = ☐

3 3 × 4 = ☐
30 × 4 = ☐

2 5 × 5 = 25
50 × 5 = ☐

4 7 × 8 = ☐
70 × 8 = ☐

Use your times tables to work out:

5 90 × 2
6 40 × 5
7 70 × 4
8 80 × 8
9 100 × 3

10 8 × 90
11 4 × 100
12 120 × 5
13 110 × 8
14 120 × 4

A tennis ball weighs 60 g.
What is the total weight of:

15 three tennis balls?
16 five tennis balls?
17 eight tennis balls?

Find the missing values in these divisions:

18 12 ÷ 2 = 6
120 ÷ 2 = ☐

20 28 ÷ 4 = ☐
280 ÷ 4 = ☐

19 18 ÷ 3 = 6
180 ÷ 3 = ☐

21 64 ÷ 8 = ☐
640 ÷ 8 = ☐

Use your times tables to work out:

22 60 ÷ 2
23 200 ÷ 5
24 160 ÷ 4
25 320 ÷ 8

26 210 ÷ 3
27 240 ÷ 4
28 880 ÷ 8
29 600 ÷ 5

30 Four identical chocolate bars weigh 360 g.
How much does one chocolate bar weigh?

31 Eight coaches are all carrying
the same number of passengers.
There are 480 passengers in total.
How many are on each coach?

Use the number lines to work out:

32 64 ÷ 4

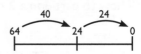

33 48 ÷ 3

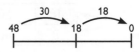

34 56 ÷ 2

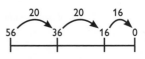

35 81 ÷ 3

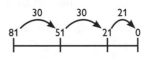

Use chunking to work out:

36 72 ÷ 2
37 80 ÷ 5
38 63 ÷ 3
39 88 ÷ 4

40 84 ÷ 3
41 104 ÷ 4
42 105 ÷ 3
43 132 ÷ 4

Use doubling to work out these multiplications:

44 13 × 4
45 16 × 4
46 14 × 8

47 75 × 4
48 21 × 8
49 35 × 8

Use halving to work out these divisions:

50 68 ÷ 4
51 116 ÷ 4
52 280 ÷ 8

53 120 ÷ 4
54 440 ÷ 8
55 488 ÷ 8

Use doubling and halving to
find the missing numbers:

56 ☐ ÷ 8 = 25
57 ☐ × 4 = 72
58 ☐ × 4 = 96

59 ☐ ÷ 8 = 15
60 ☐ ÷ 4 = 31
61 ☐ ÷ 8 = 41

Phew, that was a lot of mental maths — well done for getting through it!

Grid Method Multiplication

If you can't do a multiplication easily in your head then you can turn to the grid method for help.
Remind yourself how to partition a 2-digit number into tens and ones before you give it a go.

Examples

Work out 18 × 5.

×	5
10	50
8	40
	90

This is 18 partitioned into tens and ones.

This is 10 × 5
This is 8 × 5

Add up the numbers you've found — this is 50 + 40.

Work out 36 × 4.

×	4
30	120
6	24
	144

This is 36 partitioned into tens and ones.

This is 30 × 4
This is 6 × 4

Add up the numbers you've found — this is 120 + 24.

Set A

Copy and complete the grid to work out:

1 15 × 4

×	4
10	
5	

2 16 × 3

×	3
10	
6	

3 23 × 5

×	5
20	
3	

4 37 × 5

×	5
30	
7	

5 24 × 8

×	8
20	
4	

6 28 × 4

×	4
20	
8	

Use the grid method to work out:

7 19 × 3   **8** 28 × 5   **9** 52 × 3   **10** 43 × 4   **11** 33 × 4   **12** 37 × 8

Set B

Copy and complete the grid to work out:

1 26 × 5

×	5
20	
6	

2 34 × 8

×	8
30	
4	

3 54 × 3

×	3
4	

4 58 × 4

×	4

5 44 × 8

×	

6 68 × 3

×	

Use the grid method to work out:

7 38 × 3   **8** 46 × 4   **9** 73 × 5   **10** 78 × 4   **11** 48 × 8   **12** 26 × 8

Set C

Copy and complete the grid to work out:

1 38 × 5

×	5
8	

2 46 × 3

×	3
40	

3 62 × 4

×	4

4 87 × 8

×	

5 122 × 4

×	
100	

6 124 × 8

×	

Use the grid method to work out:

7 84 × 3   **8** 96 × 8   **9** 75 × 3   **10** 76 × 4   **11** 158 × 3   **12** 119 × 8

I can multiply using the grid method.

    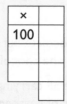

Short Multiplication

You can also multiply 2-digit numbers by 1-digit numbers using short multiplication.
Just make sure you line up the digits in place value columns first.

Examples

Work out 32 × 3.

```
    3  2
×      3
───────
    9  6
```

Line up the ones digits in the same place value column.

Work out 16 × 3.

```
    1  6
×      3
───────
    4  8
    1
```

6 × 3 = 18, so 1 ten is carried to the tens column.

Work out 61 × 8.

```
    6  1
×      8
───────
  4  8  8
  4
```

60 × 8 = 480, so 4 hundreds are carried to the hundreds column.

Set A

Work out:

1.
```
    1  3
×      2
```

2.
```
    2  2
×      4
```

3.
```
    2  6
×      3
```

Work out:

4.
```
    1  7
×      3
```

5.
```
    2  9
×      4
```

6.
```
    1  6
×      8
```

Use short multiplication to work out:

7. 15 × 4
8. 13 × 8
9. 21 × 5
10. eighteen lots of three
11. twenty-four lots of three
12. twenty-two lots of five

Set B

Work out:

1.
```
    1  9
×      5
```

2.
```
    3  3
×      4
```

3.
```
    2  8
×      8
```

Work out:

4. 53 × 4
5. 81 × 5
6. 39 × 3
7. 47 × 4
8. 38 × 8
9. 72 × 8

Use short multiplication to work out:

10. forty-seven lots of three
11. twenty-nine lots of four

What number is:

12. 3 times bigger than 73?
13. 4 times bigger than 56?
14. 8 times bigger than 63?

Set C

Work out:

1. 52 × 4
2. 63 × 3
3. 76 × 3
4. 84 × 4
5. 53 × 8
6. 78 × 8

What number is:

7. 3 times bigger than 88?
8. 4 times bigger than 56?
9. 3 times bigger than 79?
10. 8 times bigger than 58?
11. 4 times bigger than 87?
12. 8 times bigger than 94?

Use short multiplication to work out:

13. sixty-seven lots of three
14. eighty-five lots of four
15. seventy-nine lots of eight

Work out:

16. 162 × 3
17. 124 × 8

I can multiply using short multiplication.

Short Division

Short division is a quick written method to answer division questions. These examples show you how it's done.

Examples

What is 69 ÷ 3?

$$\begin{array}{r} \mathbf{2\ 3} \\ 3\ \overline{\smash{)}6\ 9} \end{array}$$ So 69 ÷ 3 = **23**.

Use short division to work out a third of 57.

$$\begin{array}{r} \mathbf{1\ 9} \\ 3\ \overline{\smash{)}5\ {}^2 7} \end{array}$$ So 57 ÷ 3 = **19**.

5 ÷ 3 = 1 remainder 2.
2 tens are exchanged for 20 ones.

Set A

Work out:

1. 2 | 4 8
2. 2 | 6 6
3. 3 | 3 9
4. 3 | 6 3
5. 4 | 8 8

Work out:

6. 5 | 8 5
7. 4 | 6 8
8. 3 | 4 8
9. 4 | 7 2
10. 4 | 9 6

Use short division to work out:

11. 62 ÷ 2
12. 78 ÷ 2
13. 92 ÷ 4
14. 51 ÷ 3
15. 56 ÷ 4
16. 95 ÷ 5

Set B

Work out:

1. 2 | 8 4
2. 3 | 9 6
3. 4 | 6 0
4. 4 | 7 6
5. 3 | 7 8

Use short division to work out:

6. 84 ÷ 4
7. 74 ÷ 2
8. 70 ÷ 5
9. 54 ÷ 3
10. 81 ÷ 3
11. 64 ÷ 4

Find the missing numbers using short division:

12. ☐ × 2 = 96
13. ☐ × 3 = 87
14. 5 × ☐ = 90
15. ☐ × 4 = 68
16. 4 × ☐ = 96

Set C

Use short division to work out:

1. 52 ÷ 2
2. 75 ÷ 5
3. 72 ÷ 3
4. 72 ÷ 4
5. 84 ÷ 3
6. 92 ÷ 4

Use short division to work out:

7. a half of 78
8. a third of 48
9. a quarter of 68
10. a third of 87
11. a fifth of 90
12. a quarter of 96

Are these statements true or false?

13. 81 ÷ 3 = 29
14. 80 ÷ 5 = 16
15. 76 ÷ 4 = 57 ÷ 3

Use short division to work out:

16. 168 ÷ 4
17. 864 ÷ 8

I can divide using short division.

Multiplication and Division Problems — 1

Here are a whole bunch of word problems to help you brush up on those problem solving skills.
The key to these questions is picking out the important bits of information and deciding which operation to use.

Examples

27 fish are divided equally between 3 fishbowls.
How many fish are in each fishbowl?

$27 \div 3 = \mathbf{9}$
So there will be **9 fish** in each fishbowl.

Caley has 50 apples. Each apple contains 8 seeds.
How many seeds are there in total?

$5 \times 8 = 40$
$50 \times 8 = \mathbf{400}$
So there are **400 seeds** in total.

There are 92 trees in an orchard.
The trees are in four equal length rows.

How many trees are in each row?

The calculation you need to do is $92 \div 4$.

$$4 \overline{\smash{)}9\,{}^{1}2} \quad \begin{matrix} 2\ 3 \end{matrix}$$

So there are **23 trees** in each row.

Set A

Zeb and Zak share some 5p coins between them.

1. Zeb gets 8 coins.
   How much money does he get?

2. Zak gets 50p. How many coins did he get?

Sam uses 3 eggs to make a cake.
How many eggs are needed to make:

3. 7 cakes?

4. 11 cakes?

How many cakes can she make with:

5. 9 eggs?

6. 27 eggs?

Joanna is 6 years old.

7. Her sister is 3 times older than her.
   How old is her sister?

8. Joanna's mum is twice as old as her sister.
   How old is her mum?

A toothbrush weighs 20 g. How much will:

9. 3 toothbrushes weigh?

10. 5 toothbrushes weigh?

11. 8 toothbrushes weigh?

12. There are 140 pupils in Year 3.
    Half of them are boys.
    How many boys are in Year 3?

4 people can sit on a park bench.

13. How many people can sit on 9 park benches?

14. If 80 people can sit on benches in a park,
    how many benches are there?

15. 5 identical biscuits weigh 150 g.
    How much does each biscuit weigh?

16. Each CD in Monib's collection has
    8 songs on it. How many songs
    are there on 14 of his CDs?

Set B

1. There are 8 cows in a field.
   There are 6 times as many sheep as cows.
   How many sheep are in the field?

2. 48 crayons are shared equally
   between 4 children.
   How many crayons does each child get?

Kylie is baking some muffins. She puts 4 blueberries and 3 raspberries on the top of each muffin.

3. How many blueberries
   will there be on 9 muffins?

4. How many raspberries
   will there be on 11 muffins?

5. Kylie uses 60 raspberries.
   How many muffins did she make?

6. Padma spends 10 minutes doing maths homework.
   She spends 4 times longer watching TV.
   How long does she spend watching TV?

7. Charlie makes 8 pizzas for a party.
   Each pizza is cut into 9 slices.
   How many slices of pizza are there?

8. Eight identical yo-yos weigh 560 g.
   How much does each yo-yo weigh?

Notebooks are sold in packs of four.

9. Alan buys 33 packs of notebooks.
   How many notebooks does he buy?

10. Mrs Cox needs 76 notebooks for her class.
    How many packs should she buy?

11. A plane has eight seats in each row.
    How many seats are there in 54 rows?

12. 81 magazines are split into three equal piles.
    How many magazines are in each pile?

13. A sandwich shop has four different types
    of bread and nine different fillings. How
    many different sandwiches can they make?

Set C

1. 11 pigeons each lay three eggs.
   How many eggs are there in total?

Jordan walks four miles every day.

2. How many miles does he walk in 20 days?

3. How many days will it take him
   to walk 200 miles?

A strip of wallpaper is 70 cm wide.
How wide are:

4. three strips of wallpaper?

5. eight strips of wallpaper?

6. 240 footballs are shared equally
   between eight different football teams.
   How many footballs does each team get?

7. 87 dance students are split equally
   into three dance groups.
   How many students are in each group?

A variety pack of cereal contains eight boxes.
How many boxes will there be in:

8. 40 packs?

9. 60 packs?

10. 74 packs?

How many variety packs would be needed for:

11. 184 boxes?

12. 432 boxes?

13. In a small bag of peanuts there are 78 nuts.
    How many nuts will there be in four bags?

14. Emily has six different football shirts and
    eight different pairs of shorts. How many
    different football kits could she wear?

15. The bookcase in Alf's house has
    eight shelves. Each shelf is 34 cm tall.
    How tall is the bookcase?

I can solve multiplication and division problems.

Multiplication and Division Problems — 2

The time has come to tackle some trickier word problems. These ones have more than one step — start off by deciding which operations you'll need to use then work out which order to do them.

Examples

Laura buys 5 gold stickers and 4 pink stickers. Stickers cost 8p each. How much does she spend?

She buys 5 + 4 = 9 stickers.

So she spends 9 × 8 = **72p**.

Trish has 3 oranges. She cuts each orange into 8 chunks and shares them equally between her 4 children. How many chunks does each child get?

She cuts the oranges into 3 × 8 = 24 chunks.

So each child gets 24 ÷ 4 = **6 chunks**.

There are 21 biscuits in a pack. Jasmine splits 4 packs of biscuits equally between 3 plates. How many biscuits are on each plate?

Start off by working out the number of biscuits:

```
  2 1
×   4
─────
  8 4
```

Then work out how many are on each plate:

```
  2 8
3 8 ²4
```

So there are **28 biscuits** on each plate.

Set A

Every crayon weighs 8 g.
What would be the total weight of:

1. 3 blue crayons and 2 green crayons?

2. 5 red crayons and 6 orange crayons?

3. There are 26 girls and 22 boys on a school trip. They are split equally between 4 minibuses. How many children are on each minibus?

4. Marta buys five boxes of 3 golf balls. She loses 7 golf balls. How many does she have left?

Tickets at the local cinema cost £8 for an adult and £4 for a child. How much would it cost for:

5. 5 children and 1 adult?

6. 4 adults and 1 child?

7. 2 adults and 2 children?

8. A teacher buys 4 boxes of 6 rubbers. She gives half of them to her class. How many rubbers does she have left?

9. 9 carrots are each cut into 4 pieces. The pieces are shared equally between 3 rabbits. How many pieces of carrot does each rabbit get?

Shiva mixes 130 ml of orange juice and 190 ml of apple juice. How much juice is in each glass if she splits the mixture between:

10. 4 glasses?

11. 8 glasses?

Teabags come in boxes of 80. A cafe uses 2 teabags in each pot of tea. How many pots of tea can they make if they buy:

12. 3 boxes of teabags?

13. 10 boxes of teabags?

There are 6 chapters in a book. Each chapter is 8 pages long. How many pages does Chloe need to read each day to finish the book in:

1. 3 days?

2. 4 days?

There are 50 boys and 46 girls in Year 3. How many tables are needed for lunch if there are:

3. 3 children at each table?

4. 8 children at each table?

5. Daisy the cow is given 45 carrots and 13 parsnips. She eats a third of the carrots and all the parsnips. How many of the vegetables does she eat in total?

6. Kobe's maths homework took him 14 minutes. His English homework took three times longer. How long did it take him to do both his maths and English homework in total?

7. Football stickers come in packs of eight. Shiva buys 50 packs and splits them equally between her four sons. How many stickers does each son get?

A chef uses three eggs to make an omelette. He buys eggs in boxes of 18. How many omelettes can he make with:

8. four boxes of eggs?

9. five boxes of eggs?

10. ten boxes of eggs?

There are 19 blue cars in a car park.

11. There are four times as many black cars as blue cars. How many black and blue cars are there altogether?

12. There are eight times as many red cars as blue cars. How many more red cars than blue cars are there?

A puzzle book has 18 puzzles in it. Sophie does 4 puzzles each day. How many days would:

1. 2 puzzle books last her?

2. 8 puzzle books last her?

3. Ivana has 450 ml of milk. She drinks 120 ml and splits the remaining milk equally between three glasses. How much milk is in each glass?

A small tank can hold 40 fish and a large tank can hold 90 fish. How many fish can:

4. eight small tanks and one large tank hold?

5. one small tank and three large tanks hold?

6. four small tanks and four large tanks hold?

7. Henry buys four bags of candyfloss that each weigh 84 g. He splits the candyfloss into eight tubs. How much candyfloss is in each tub?

8. Are there more toy soldiers in eight packs of 16 soldiers or three packs of 40 soldiers?

9. A school has eight classes. Each class has 29 pupils in it. Half the pupils in the school are girls. How many pupils are girls?

Gio and Gina each get £8 pocket money every week.

10. Gio saved his pocket money for 24 weeks then spent £56. How much pocket money did he have left?

11. Gina wants to buy a train set for £90. How many weeks will she have to save her pocket money for to be able to pay for the train set?

12. Eight people can go on a theme park ride every three minutes. There are 120 people in the queue. How many minutes will it be before they've all been on the ride?

I am confident solving multiplication and division problems.

Multiplication and Division — Review 3

Copy and complete the grid to work out:

(1) 18 × 4

×	4
10	
8	

(3) 23 × 8

×	8

(2) 48 × 3

×	3
40	

(4) 62 × 8

×	

Use short multiplication to work out:

(5)
```
  1 7
×   5
```

(7)
```
  6 6
×   4
```

(6)
```
  4 3
×   3
```

(8)
```
  8 2
×   8
```

Work out:

(9) 31 × 3

(10) 37 × 2

(11) 51 × 4

(12) 62 × 3

(13) 71 × 5

(14) 42 × 8

(15) 38 × 4

(16) 77 × 3

(17) 73 × 8

(18) 92 × 8

Work out:

(19) 2 | 6 8

(20) 3 | 9 3

(21) 4 | 8 4

(22) 2 | 9 2

(23) 5 | 6 5

(24) 3 | 7 5

(25) 3 | 8 1

(26) 4 | 9 2

Use short division to work out:

(27) 54 ÷ 2

(28) 72 ÷ 3

(29) 90 ÷ 5

(30) 52 ÷ 4

(31) 76 ÷ 4

(32) 94 ÷ 2

(33) 124 ÷ 4

(34) 159 ÷ 3

A brick is 8 cm tall. How tall are:

(35) 6 bricks stacked on top of each other?

(36) 20 bricks stacked on top of each other?

(37) 31 bricks stacked on top of each other?

3 birds can nest in one birdhouse.
How many birds can nest in:

(38) 9 birdhouses?

(39) 30 birdhouses?

(40) How many birdhouses are needed
so that 42 birds can nest?

(41) A roller coaster can hold 72 people at once.
4 people can sit in each roller coaster cart.
How many carts does the roller coaster have?

(42) An ice cream shop sells 11 different flavours
of ice cream and 3 different toppings.
How many different ice creams can be ordered?

(43) Lucy buys eight packs of seven friendship
bracelets. She gives 23 bracelets to her friends.
How many bracelets does she have left?

(44) A zookeeper buys 12 packs of four kiwi fruits.
He shares the kiwi fruits equally between
three koalas. How many does each koala get?

Cars and vans both have four wheels.
How many wheels will:

(45) nine cars and three vans have?

(46) twenty cars and fifty vans have?

(47) twenty-seven cars and one van have?

(48) Bethan has £14 in her purse.
Her mum has eight times as much.
How much money do they have in total?

(49) Four scoops of mixed corn can feed
three chickens. How many chickens
will 160 scoops of mixed corn feed?

Well done for giving all those questions a go — you're a maths star!

Multiplication and Division — Challenges

 1   Lara Jones is a temple explorer. She needs to get through the rooms in a temple to find some treasure.
If she steps on a wrong floor tile, the room's exit will close.
Follow the instructions and shade the safe path through these rooms for Lara Jones.
She can only move left, right, forwards and backwards. No diagonal jumps.

Room 1: Any tile with a number in the
3 or 4 times table on it is safe.

Room 2: Any tile with a number in the
5 or 8 times table on it is safe.

ENTRANCE					
4	38	48	35	3	34
9	27	29	26	1	5
41	44	16	21	2	13
70	11	19	28	25	22
12	40	36	6	33	27
8	23	17	7	10	19
EXIT					

ENTRANCE					
64	1	17	69	73	15
11	20	88	16	31	60
18	48	12	8	32	56
96	30	28	36	41	4
22	25	40	45	24	9
72	7	34	5	66	74
EXIT					

 2   a) Follow the instructions on these calculation machines to fill in the missing numbers.

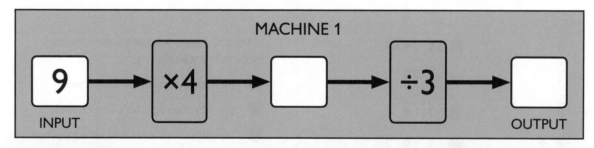

MACHINE 1

9 → ×4 → ☐ → ÷3 → ☐

INPUT   OUTPUT

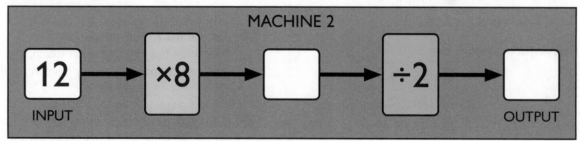

MACHINE 2

12 → ×8 → ☐ → ÷2 → ☐

INPUT   OUTPUT

b) Try putting some different numbers into machine 2 (for example, 1, 2, 3, 4 and 5).
Can you find a pattern between the input and the output of the machine?
Can you explain why this pattern happens?

3 a) Can you work out what number each person is thinking of?

If you multiply my number by 8, you get 96.

Neil

If you halve my number and then multiply the answer by 8, you get 88.

Megan

If you double my number twice and then divide by 8, you get 4.

Alia

If you multiply my number by 4 and then divide the answer by 3, you get 8.

Habib

b) Make up some of your own "thinking of a number" questions and test them out on your friends.

4 Put the digits 3, 4 and 8 into the calculation below to find as many different answers as you can. There are six to find in total.

5 A bar of chocolate is made up of 20 square pieces shown in the pattern below.

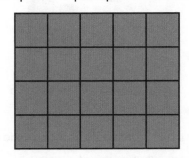

a) Draw two more possible rectangular patterns that can be made with 20 square pieces.

b) How many different rectangles could you make out of 48 square pieces of chocolate?

c) Could you make more squares and rectangles if you had 64 tiles instead of 48? Explain your answer.

6   On the planet Neptuleon, there are two types of monster.

Steppers have 3 eyes.   Sliders have 5 eyes.

a)   How many eyes would 9 steppers and 6 sliders have in total?

b)   How many eyes would 80 steppers and 20 sliders have in total?

c)   Space Commander Rex captures some steppers and sliders.
     They have 18 eyes in total. How many steppers and sliders do you think he captured?

d)   Space Commander Leona also captures some steppers and sliders.
     They have 28 eyes in total. How many steppers and sliders do you think she captured?
     Can you think of another possible answer?

7   Now it's your turn to write the questions and test your friends.

Write your own question for each of the multiplications and divisions below.
Try to think of some really fun stories and settings for your questions.
Once you're happy with your questions give them to a friend to try and solve.

$$9 \times 4 \qquad 72 \div 8 \qquad 20 \times 3 \qquad 400 \div 4$$

8   Zoe has some pictures that she wants to divide into photo albums.

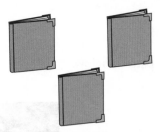 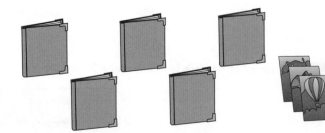

When she divides the pictures between   When she divides the pictures
3 albums, she doesn't have any left over.   between 5 albums, she has 3 left over.

a)   If Zoe has less than 20 pictures, how many pictures do you think she has?

b)   If Zoe has more than 20 pictures, can you find some other numbers of pictures that Zoe could have?

You've reached the end of the section — hope you enjoyed all those tricky challenges!

Fractions

Fractions are equal parts of a whole object or number — you can show fractions by shading in parts of a shape or by using a number line.

Example

What fraction of the shape below is shaded?

The shape has 4 equal parts. 3 of them are shaded.

So 3 out of 4 or $\frac{3}{4}$ of the shape is shaded.

Set A

What fraction of each shape has been shaded?

1

2

3

4

Copy the shape and shade the fraction shown:

5 $\frac{1}{2}$

6 $\frac{1}{4}$

7 $\frac{4}{5}$

8 $\frac{1}{8}$

9 Copy out the number line below.

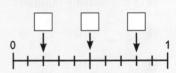

Use the fractions below to fill in the gaps.

$$\frac{5}{10} \qquad \frac{8}{10} \qquad \frac{2}{10}$$

Set B

What fraction of each shape has been shaded?

1

2

3

Identify the fractions on the number lines below:

4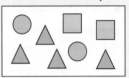

5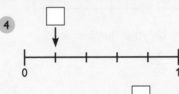

Look at the box of shapes below.

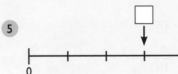

What fraction of the shapes are:

6 circles?

7 triangles?

8 not squares?

Set C

Copy the shapes below.

A   B   C

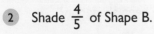

1 Shade $\frac{2}{4}$ of Shape A.

2 Shade $\frac{4}{5}$ of Shape B.

3 Shade $\frac{3}{8}$ of Shape C.

A circle is divided into eight equal parts.

What fraction of the circle is shaded if:

4 five parts are shaded?

5 all but one part is shaded?

6 every shaded part is between two non-shaded parts?

Look at each shape below.

 "$\frac{2}{3}$ of this shape is shaded."

7 Explain why this is wrong.

 "$\frac{1}{3}$ of this shape is shaded."

8 Explain why this is wrong.

I understand what fractions are.

Dividing with Tenths

If you divide an object into 10 equal parts, each part is 1 tenth of the whole object.
You can divide numbers like this too — if you divide a number by 10, you're just finding 1 tenth of that number.

Examples

Jamal divides a pie into 10 equal slices.
He eats three slices.

How many tenths of the pie does he eat?

Each slice is 1 tenth of the whole pie.
So he eats **three tenths** of the pie.

What is $2 \div 10$?

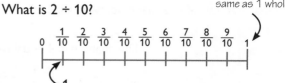

ten tenths is the same as 1 whole

$1 \div 10 = \dfrac{1}{10}$ (one part of the number line)

$2 \div 10$ is the same as two parts $= \dfrac{2}{10}$

Set A

Find the missing numbers:

1. $\boxed{} \div 10 = \dfrac{3}{10}$

2. $\boxed{} \div 10 = \dfrac{8}{10}$

3. $7 \div 10 = \dfrac{\boxed{}}{\boxed{}}$

4. $9 \div 10 = \dfrac{\boxed{}}{\boxed{}}$

Look at the shapes below.

Which shape shows:

5. two tenths?

6. nine tenths?

A cake is divided into 10 equal slices.

Janice and Skylar eat three slices each.
Keira eats four slices.

How many tenths
of the cake does:

7. Janice eat?

8. Skylar eat?

9. Keira eat?

Set B

What fraction of each
shape has been shaded?

1.

2.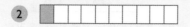

3.

4.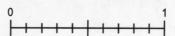

Copy the number line below.

Mark on your number line:

5. $\dfrac{2}{10}$

6. $\dfrac{4}{10}$

7. $\dfrac{9}{10}$

Look at the box of shapes below.

True or false?

8. $4 \div 10$ gives the fraction of
shapes that are triangles.

9. $3 \div 10$ gives the fraction of
shapes that are not circles.

Set C

Work out, giving your
answer as a fraction:

1. five divided by ten

2. four divided by ten

Work out, giving your
answer in words:

3. $8 \div 10$

4. $3 \div 10$

Copy the number line below.

Write as a fraction, and then
mark on your number line:

5. $1 \div 10$

6. $7 \div 10$

7. $6 \div 10$

The shapes below are
divided into equal parts.

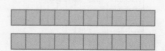

8. How many tenths
have been shaded in?

9. Explain how the diagram
shows that 20 tenths = 2.

I can find tenths of objects and amounts.

Counting in Tenths

If you find it tricky counting up and down in tenths, it might help to draw a number line.
Look at the example below and have a go at some questions yourself.

You can count over one whole.
This is "one and one tenth".

Example

Starting at $\frac{4}{10}$, count forward 5 steps of $\frac{1}{10}$.

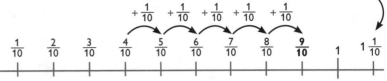

You might want to use this number line to help you answer the questions below. Each gap is one tenth.

Set A

Starting at 0, count forward:

1 2 steps of $\frac{1}{10}$

2 4 steps of $\frac{1}{10}$

Starting at $\frac{9}{10}$, count back:

3 3 steps of $\frac{1}{10}$

4 6 steps of $\frac{1}{10}$

The lines below are split into tenths.
Count forward to find the missing value:

5

6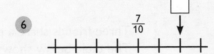

How many tenths are there:

7 between $\frac{1}{10}$ and $\frac{4}{10}$?

8 between $\frac{6}{10}$ and $\frac{8}{10}$?

9 between $\frac{3}{10}$ and $\frac{7}{10}$?

10 between $\frac{9}{10}$ and 1?

11 between 0 and 1?

Set B

Starting at $\frac{6}{10}$, count:

1 forward 1 tenth

2 forward 3 tenths

3 back 4 tenths

4 forward 1 tenth, then back 2 tenths

5 forward 4 tenths, then back 6 tenths

The lines below are split into tenths.
Count back to find the missing value:

6

7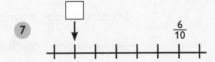

The shape below is divided into 10 equal parts.

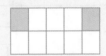

How many more parts should be shaded to show:

8 $\frac{5}{10}$?

9 $\frac{8}{10}$?

Set C

Starting at 1, count:

1 back 5 tenths

2 forward 2 tenths

3 forward 7 tenths

4 forward 1 tenth, then back 2 tenths

5 forward 4 tenths, then back 6 tenths

Copy the number line below.

Mark on your number line:

6 $1\frac{1}{10}$

7 $1\frac{9}{10}$

8 one and three tenths

9 one and six tenths

Both shapes below are divided into 10 equal parts.

How many fewer parts should be shaded to show:

10 one whole?

11 $\frac{7}{10}$?

I can count up and down in tenths.

What fraction of each shape has been shaded?

①    ④

②   ⑤

③   ⑥

Copy the shape and shade the fraction shown:

⑦ $\frac{3}{5}$

⑧ $\frac{7}{8}$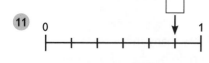

⑨ $\frac{2}{6}$

Identify the fractions on the number lines below:

⑩ 0 ↓ 1

⑪ 0 ↓ 1

⑫ 0 ↓ 1

⑬ Look at the shape below.

"Three quarters of this shape is shaded."

Is this true?
Explain your answer.

Find the missing numbers:

⑭ $2 \div \boxed{} = \frac{2}{10}$ ⑯ $\frac{\boxed{}}{10} = 1$

⑮ $\boxed{} \div 10 = \frac{9}{10}$ ⑰ $3 \div 10 = \frac{\boxed{}}{\boxed{}}$

Copy the number line below.

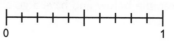
0   1

Mark on your number line:

⑱ $\frac{3}{10}$ ⑳ $\frac{8}{10}$

⑲ five tenths   ㉑ ten tenths

Look at the box of letters on the right.

What fraction of the total letters:

㉒ are the letter A?

㉓ are not the letter D?

Three friends share a pizza. They cut it into 10 slices. The table below shows the number of slices they each eat.

	Slices eaten
Tamsyn	5
Alex	2
Miro	3

㉔ What fraction of the pizza did Miro eat?

㉕ Who ate two tenths of pizza more than Miro?

Starting at $\frac{7}{10}$, count:

㉖ forward 1 tenth   ㉚ forward 7 tenths, then back 3 tenths

㉗ forward 4 tenths   ㉛ forward 6 tenths, then back 5 tenths

㉘ back 2 tenths

㉙ back 5 tenths

Look at the number line below.

A   B   C   D
0   1   2

What fraction do you get if you count:

㉜ forward 2 tenths from A   ㉞ forward 4 tenths from C

㉝ back 7 tenths from B   ㉟ back 10 tenths from D

Excellent work — you'll be a whizz with fractions in no time!

Equivalent Fractions

'Equivalent' might look like a scary word, but it just means 'equal'.
Shading fraction bars will help you find two fractions that are equivalent.

Examples

Shade the circles below to show that $\frac{1}{2}$ and $\frac{2}{4}$ are equal.

Show $\frac{1}{2}$ on this circle:

divide into 2 equal parts and shade 1 of them.

Show $\frac{2}{4}$ on this circle:

divide into 4 equal parts and shade 2 of them.

The same amount is shaded on each circle, so $\frac{1}{2}$ and $\frac{2}{4}$ are equal.

Draw fraction bars to find the missing number: $\frac{2}{3} = \frac{\square}{6}$

Divide a rectangle into 3 equal parts and shade in 2 parts to show $\frac{2}{3}$.

Make each 'fraction bar' the same width.

Divide a second rectangle into 6 equal parts. Shading in 4 parts matches the amount shaded on the first rectangle.

This tells you that $\frac{2}{3} = \frac{4}{6}$

Set A

Copy and shade the second shape so the fraction shaded is the same as in the first shape. Then write down the equivalent fractions shown by each pair.

1

2

3

4

5

6

The rectangle below is divided into 6 equal parts.

7 How many sixths of this shape are shaded?

Look at this box of fractions:

$$\frac{1}{2} \quad \frac{1}{3} \quad \frac{1}{4} \quad \frac{1}{5}$$

8 Which fraction from the box also shows how much of the shape is shaded?

The square below is divided into 8 equal parts.

Two parts are shaded.

Complete the sentences:

9 The square has $\frac{\square}{8}$ shaded.

10 The square has $\frac{\square}{4}$ shaded.

Set B

For each pair of shapes, say whether they have an equal or different fraction shaded.

Write down any fractions that are equal.

1

2

3

4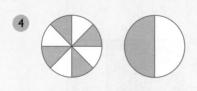

5

The shape below is divided into 12 equal parts.

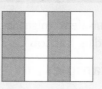

Complete the sentences:

6 ▢/12 of the shape is shaded.

7 ▢/2 of the shape is shaded.

8 ▢/6 of the shape is shaded.

Copy each of the shapes below.

Shape A   Shape B

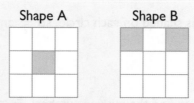

Shade in more squares so that:

9 $\frac{1}{3}$ of Shape A is shaded.

10 $\frac{2}{3}$ of Shape B is shaded.

Set C

Copy the shape and shade in the fraction shown:

1 one half

2 one third

3 two quarters

4 one fifth

5 two fifths

6 four sixths

Draw fraction bars to help you answer the questions below.

Complete the sentences:

7 ▢/8 is the same as $\frac{1}{2}$.

8 ▢/8 is the same as $\frac{3}{4}$.

Look at the fractions in the box below.

$\frac{2}{10}$	$\frac{1}{3}$	$\frac{1}{8}$	$\frac{1}{4}$	$\frac{3}{6}$

Which fraction from the box is equal to:

9 $\frac{1}{5}$

10 $\frac{2}{8}$

11 $\frac{1}{2}$

12 $\frac{3}{9}$

I can recognise and show equivalent fractions.

Ordering Fractions — 1

It's easy to compare two fractions with the same denominator (bottom number) — if the numerator (top number) is bigger, then that fraction is bigger too.

Example

Order the fractions in the box, from largest to smallest.

$$\frac{3}{6} \quad \frac{5}{6} \quad \frac{2}{6} \quad \frac{1}{6}$$

All the bottom numbers are the same.

Look at the top numbers:
5 is largest, then 3, 2 and 1.

So the correct order is $\frac{5}{6}$, $\frac{3}{6}$, $\frac{2}{6}$, $\frac{1}{6}$

Check your answer with fraction bars:

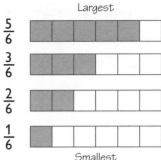

Largest

$\frac{5}{6}$

$\frac{3}{6}$

$\frac{2}{6}$

$\frac{1}{6}$

Smallest

Set A

Copy the fraction bars below and shade the amounts shown.

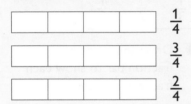

$\frac{1}{4}$

$\frac{3}{4}$

$\frac{2}{4}$

1. Which is the largest fraction?

2. Which is the smallest fraction?

Which is the larger fraction:

3. $\frac{1}{3}$ or $\frac{2}{3}$?

4. $\frac{3}{5}$ or $\frac{2}{5}$?

5. $\frac{2}{8}$ or $\frac{1}{8}$?

6. $\frac{3}{9}$ or $\frac{5}{9}$?

7. $\frac{2}{10}$ or $\frac{5}{10}$?

Look at the fractions in the box:

$$\frac{3}{5} \quad \frac{4}{5} \quad \frac{1}{5}$$

8. Draw and shade a fraction bar to show each fraction from the box.

9. Use your fraction bars to order the fractions, from largest to smallest.

Set B

Which symbol (< or >) should go in each box?

1. $\frac{1}{6} \square \frac{4}{6}$

2. $\frac{2}{10} \square \frac{9}{10}$

3. $\frac{3}{5} \square \frac{1}{5}$

4. $\frac{6}{8} \square \frac{2}{8}$

5. $\frac{3}{6} \square \frac{5}{6}$

Order these fractions, from smallest to largest:

6. $$\frac{1}{4} \quad \frac{3}{4} \quad \frac{2}{4}$$

7. $$\frac{4}{5} \quad \frac{2}{5} \quad \frac{1}{5} \quad \frac{3}{5}$$

8. $$\frac{2}{8} \quad \frac{7}{8} \quad \frac{1}{8} \quad \frac{5}{8}$$

Look at these four digits:

6 1 5 4

Pick a digit to complete each sentence below:

9. $\frac{3}{5}$ is bigger than $\frac{\square}{5}$.

10. $\frac{\square}{6}$ is smaller than five sixths, and is bigger than two sixths.

Set C

Order these fractions, from largest to smallest:

1. $$\frac{1}{4} \quad \frac{3}{4} \quad \frac{2}{4} \quad \frac{4}{4}$$

2. $$\frac{2}{12} \quad \frac{5}{12} \quad \frac{11}{12} \quad \frac{8}{12}$$

3. $$\frac{7}{8} \quad \frac{5}{8} \quad \frac{2}{8} \quad \frac{1}{8} \quad \frac{3}{8}$$

What fraction is halfway between:

4. $\frac{1}{4}$ and $\frac{3}{4}$?

5. $\frac{2}{5}$ and $\frac{4}{5}$?

6. $\frac{3}{8}$ and $\frac{5}{8}$?

7. 0 and $\frac{2}{12}$?

8. $\frac{4}{6}$ and 1 ?

Three friends recorded how far they jogged in a week:

- Carlos jogged $\frac{2}{8}$ of a mile.

- Khalid jogged $\frac{7}{8}$ of a mile.

- Dennis jogged $\frac{5}{8}$ of a mile.

9. Who jogged the furthest?

10. Write a distance further than Dennis's distance but less than Khalid's.

I can compare and order fractions with the same denominator.

Ordering Fractions — 2

Unit fractions are fractions with a **1** at the top. To compare two unit fractions look at the denominators (bottom numbers) — the one with the bigger denominator is the smaller fraction.

Example

Use fraction bars to show that $\frac{1}{3}$ is bigger than $\frac{1}{4}$.

$\frac{1}{4}$

$\frac{1}{3}$

Both of these fractions are unit fractions because they have a 1 at the top.

This part is bigger.

Set A

Draw fraction bars to work out which is the smaller fraction:

1. $\frac{1}{2}$ or $\frac{1}{4}$

2. $\frac{1}{3}$ or $\frac{1}{6}$

3. $\frac{1}{5}$ or $\frac{1}{3}$

4. $\frac{1}{2}$ or $\frac{1}{3}$

Which is the larger fraction:

5. $\frac{1}{2}$ or $\frac{1}{5}$?

6. $\frac{1}{6}$ or $\frac{1}{10}$?

7. $\frac{1}{3}$ or $\frac{1}{2}$?

8. $\frac{1}{4}$ or $\frac{1}{3}$?

9. $\frac{1}{6}$ or $\frac{1}{8}$?

Look at the fractions in the box:

$$\frac{1}{3} \qquad \frac{1}{2} \qquad \frac{1}{5}$$

10. Draw and shade a fraction bar to show each fraction from the box.

11. Use your fraction bars to order the fractions, from largest to smallest.

Set B

Which symbol (< or >) should go in each box?

1. $\frac{1}{6}$ ☐ $\frac{1}{2}$

2. $\frac{1}{8}$ ☐ $\frac{1}{5}$

3. $\frac{1}{3}$ ☐ $\frac{1}{6}$

4. $\frac{1}{10}$ ☐ $\frac{1}{12}$

5. $\frac{1}{5}$ ☐ $\frac{1}{9}$

Order these fractions, from smallest to largest:

6. $\frac{1}{4} \quad \frac{1}{8} \quad \frac{1}{3}$

7. $\frac{1}{2} \quad \frac{1}{10} \quad \frac{1}{6}$

8. $\frac{1}{7} \quad \frac{1}{3} \quad \frac{1}{9} \quad \frac{1}{5}$

Look at these four digits:

$$\boxed{3} \quad \boxed{6} \quad \boxed{1} \quad \boxed{5}$$

Pick a digit to complete each sentence below:

9. $\frac{1}{5}$ is bigger than $\frac{1}{\boxed{}}$.

10. $\frac{1}{\boxed{}}$ is smaller than one half, and is bigger than one quarter.

Set C

Order these fractions, from largest to smallest:

1. $\frac{1}{7} \quad \frac{1}{9} \quad \frac{1}{2} \quad \frac{1}{10}$

2. $\frac{1}{5} \quad \frac{1}{6} \quad \frac{1}{12} \quad \frac{1}{2}$

3. $\frac{1}{8} \quad \frac{1}{3} \quad \frac{1}{10} \quad \frac{1}{6} \quad \frac{1}{4}$

Look at the number line below.

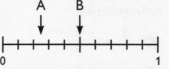

Rewrite the sentences with 'bigger' or 'smaller' in each gap:

4. $\frac{1}{5}$ is ☐ than A and B.

5. $\frac{1}{3}$ is ☐ than A and ☐ than B.

6. One eighth of the blocks in a tower are blue and one tenth are red.

Are there more red or blue blocks in the tower?

7. String A is half as long as String C. String B is a third as long as String C.

Order strings A, B and C from shortest to longest.

I can compare and order unit fractions.

Fractions — Review 2

Copy and shade the second shape so the fraction shaded is the same as in the first shape. Then write down the equivalent fractions shown by each pair.

(1)

(2)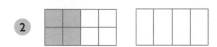

(3)

(4)

Look at the two shapes below.

A   B

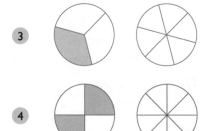

Complete the sentences:

(5) $\frac{\square}{6}$ or $\frac{\square}{2}$ of Shape A is shaded.

(6) $\frac{\square}{9}$ or $\frac{\square}{3}$ of Shape B is shaded.

(7) The shape below is split into eight equal parts.

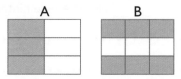

Jordan shades six squares.

Complete the sentence:

"Jordan shades $\frac{\square}{8}$ or $\frac{\square}{4}$ of the shape."

Look at the fractions in the box below.

| $\frac{1}{10}$ | $\frac{1}{3}$ | $\frac{1}{5}$ | $\frac{1}{8}$ | $\frac{1}{2}$ | $\frac{1}{4}$ |

Choose a fraction from the box that is equal to:

(8) $\frac{2}{10}$

(9) $\frac{5}{10}$

(10) $\frac{2}{6}$

(11) $\frac{2}{8}$

(12) Copy the fraction bars and shade the amounts shown.

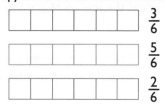

$\frac{3}{6}$

$\frac{5}{6}$

$\frac{2}{6}$

Which fraction is the smallest?

Which is the largest fraction:

(13) $\frac{2}{3}$ or $\frac{3}{3}$?

(14) $\frac{6}{7}$ or $\frac{2}{7}$?

(15) $\frac{1}{8}$ or $\frac{5}{8}$?

(16) $\frac{6}{10}$, $\frac{1}{10}$ or $\frac{9}{10}$?

Which symbol (< or >) should go in each box?

(17) $\frac{1}{3}$ ☐ $\frac{2}{3}$

(18) $\frac{3}{7}$ ☐ $\frac{6}{7}$

(19) $\frac{3}{5}$ ☐ $\frac{2}{5}$

(20) $\frac{7}{8}$ ☐ 1

Order these fractions, from smallest to largest:

(21) $\frac{4}{5}$, $\frac{2}{5}$, $\frac{3}{5}$

(22) $\frac{3}{10}$, $\frac{7}{10}$, $\frac{1}{10}$, $\frac{9}{10}$

(23) Copy the fraction bars and shade the amounts shown.

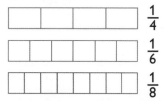

$\frac{1}{4}$

$\frac{1}{6}$

$\frac{1}{8}$

Which fraction is the smallest?

Which is the largest fraction:

(24) $\frac{1}{5}$ or $\frac{1}{8}$?

(25) $\frac{1}{6}$ or $\frac{1}{3}$?

(26) $\frac{1}{5}$ or $\frac{1}{6}$?

(27) $\frac{1}{4}$, $\frac{1}{3}$ or $\frac{1}{2}$?

(28) Look at the number line and box of fractions below.

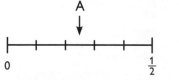 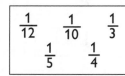

Which fractions in the box are smaller than A? Order them, from smallest to largest.

Two big thumbs up — another load of fraction questions completed!

Adding Fractions

Adding two fractions is easy-peasy if the bottom numbers of the fractions are the same — all you have to do is add the top numbers and leave the bottom number alone.

Example

What is $\frac{1}{4} + \frac{2}{4}$?

The bottom numbers are the same, so add the top numbers:

$1 + 2 = 3$, so $\frac{1}{4} + \frac{2}{4} = \frac{3}{4}$

Check your answer with fraction bars:

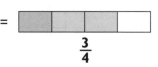

$\frac{1}{4}$ $\frac{2}{4}$ $\frac{3}{4}$

Set A

Copy and shade the final shape:

1.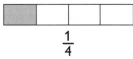

2.

3.

4.

Work out:

5. $\frac{1}{3} + \frac{1}{3}$

6. $\frac{1}{4} + \frac{1}{4}$

7. $\frac{3}{5} + \frac{1}{5}$

8. $\frac{2}{6} + \frac{3}{6}$

9. $\frac{1}{8} + \frac{2}{8}$

Find the missing words in the sentences below:

10. one third plus two thirds = ☐ thirds

11. two fifths plus ☐ fifths = four fifths

12. three ninths plus ☐ ninths = nine ninths

Set B

Copy and shade the first shape to make each calculation correct:

1.

2.

3.

4.

Work out:

5. $\frac{1}{7} + \frac{5}{7}$

6. $\frac{2}{8} + \frac{3}{8}$

7. $\frac{6}{10} + \frac{1}{10}$

8. $\frac{1}{8} + \frac{6}{8}$

9. $\frac{3}{6} + \frac{3}{6}$

10. Lindsey reads two sixths of a book on Monday and three sixths on Tuesday.

Complete the calculation below to find the total fraction of the book she reads.

$\frac{\boxed{}}{6} + \frac{\boxed{}}{6} = \frac{\boxed{}}{6}$

Set C

Copy and shade the first fraction bar to make each calculation correct:

1. ☐ + $\frac{1}{3}$ =

2. + = 1

3. + = $\frac{4}{5}$

4. + $\frac{1}{6}$ =

Find the missing values:

5. $\frac{3}{8} + \frac{\boxed{}}{8} = \frac{7}{8}$

6. $\frac{\boxed{}}{6} + \frac{4}{6} = \frac{5}{6}$

7. $\frac{\boxed{}}{9} + \frac{4}{9} = \frac{7}{9}$

8. $\frac{5}{8} + \frac{\boxed{}}{8} = 1$

Will thinks of a fraction.

He adds two fifths to his fraction and gets four fifths.

9. What fraction was he thinking of?

10. What fraction should he have started with to get one whole?

I can add fractions with the same denominator.

Subtracting Fractions

Subtracting one fraction from another is also a piece of cake if the bottom numbers are the same — subtract the top numbers and leave the bottom number alone.

Example

What is $\frac{4}{5} - \frac{3}{5}$?

The bottom numbers are the same, so subtract the top numbers:

$4 - 3 = 1$, so $\frac{4}{5} - \frac{3}{5} = \frac{1}{5}$

Check your answer with fraction bars:

$\frac{4}{5}$ — $\frac{3}{5}$ = $\frac{1}{5}$

Set A

Copy and shade the final shape:

1. ▇ − ▇ = ▢
2. ▇ − ▇ = ▢
3. ▇ − ▇ = ▢
4. ▇ − ▇ = ▢

Work out:

5. $\frac{3}{4} - \frac{2}{4}$

6. $\frac{2}{6} - \frac{1}{6}$

7. $\frac{4}{5} - \frac{2}{5}$

8. $\frac{3}{3} - \frac{1}{3}$

9. $\frac{2}{8} - \frac{1}{8}$

Work out, giving your answer in words:

10. five sixths minus two sixths

11. two fifths minus one fifth

12. one half minus one half

13. one whole minus one third

Set B

Copy and shade the first shape to make each calculation correct:

1. ▢ − ▇ = ▢
2. ▢ − ▇ = ▢
3. ▢ − ▇ = ▇
4. ▢ − ▇ = ▢

Work out:

5. $\frac{4}{5} - \frac{3}{5}$

6. $\frac{2}{7} - \frac{1}{7}$

7. $\frac{8}{10} - \frac{5}{10}$

8. $\frac{2}{3} - \frac{2}{3}$

9. $\frac{9}{10} - \frac{8}{10}$

10. Freja has eight tenths of a chocolate cake. She eats five tenths.

Complete the calculation below to find the fraction of the cake she has left.

$\frac{\square}{10} - \frac{\square}{10} = \frac{\square}{10}$

Set C

Copy and shade the blank fraction bar to make each calculation correct:

1. $\frac{2}{3}$ − ▢ = ▢
2. ▢ − ▢ = 0
3. $\frac{4}{5}$ − ▢ = ▇
4. ▢ − $\frac{3}{6}$ = ▇

Find the missing values:

5. $\frac{2}{3} - \frac{\square}{3} = \frac{1}{3}$

6. $\frac{\square}{7} - \frac{4}{7} = \frac{2}{7}$

7. $\frac{4}{5} - \frac{\square}{5} = \frac{3}{5}$

8. $\frac{\square}{8} - \frac{2}{8} = 0$

Eli has a tower of ten bricks.

He removes three tenths of the bricks in the tower.

9. What fraction of the bricks are still in the tower?

He removes another brick.

10. What fraction of the bricks are still in the tower now?

I can subtract fractions with the same denominator.

Fractions of Amounts — 1

You can find fractions of numbers or groups of objects.
On this page, you'll practice doing it with fractions that have 1 on top (unit fractions).

Example

What is $\frac{1}{5}$ of a set of 10 marbles?

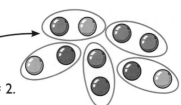

Split the 10 marbles into 5 equal groups.

Each group has **2 marbles**, so $\frac{1}{5}$ of 10 = 2.

You can also use division:

$\frac{1}{5}$ of 10 marbles = 10 ÷ 5 = **2 marbles**

When the fraction has 1 on top,
just divide by the bottom number.

Set A

Copy out the eight dots
for each question below.

Circle:

1   $\frac{1}{2}$ of the dots.

2   $\frac{1}{8}$ of the dots.

3   $\frac{1}{4}$ of the dots.

What is:

4   $\frac{1}{2}$ of 6?

5   $\frac{1}{4}$ of 8?

6   $\frac{1}{3}$ of 9?

7   $\frac{1}{10}$ of 10?

8   $\frac{1}{2}$ of 100?

Use a number from the box to
answer each question below.

| 1 | 3 | 4 | 5 | 10 | 15 |

Zara has fifteen paper cups.

One third of her cups are green.
One fifth of her cups are red.

How many paper cups are:

9   green?

10   red?

Set B

Use the picture to help you
answer the questions below.

What is:

1   $\frac{1}{6}$ of 12?

2   $\frac{1}{3}$ of 12?

3   $\frac{1}{4}$ of 12?

What is:

4   $\frac{1}{4}$ of 20?

5   $\frac{1}{5}$ of 30?

6   $\frac{1}{10}$ of 20?

7   one half of twelve?

8   one quarter of eight?

9   one eighth of eight?

Use a fraction from the box to
answer each question below.

| $\frac{1}{10}$ | $\frac{1}{5}$ | $\frac{1}{4}$ | $\frac{1}{2}$ |

Find the missing fraction:

10   $\frac{\square}{\square}$ of 20 = 10

11   $\frac{\square}{\square}$ of 20 = 4

Set C

Work out:

1   $\frac{1}{4}$ of 12

2   $\frac{1}{8}$ of 16

3   $\frac{1}{5}$ of 40

4   $\frac{1}{10}$ of 30

5   $\frac{1}{3}$ of 24

Find the missing values:

6   $\frac{1}{\square}$ of 10 = 5

7   $\frac{1}{\square}$ of 21 = 7

8   $\frac{1}{\square}$ of 30 = 6

9   $\frac{1}{\square}$ of 50 = 5

Matt starts with 40 sweets.

He gives one half of
his sweets to Anil.

Anil gives one quarter
of his sweets to Isla.

How many sweets does:

10   Matt have left?

11   Isla have?

I can find unit fractions of an amount.

Fractions of Amounts — 2

Here is some more practice with fractions of amounts, but this time the top of the fraction is bigger than 1.

Example

What is $\frac{2}{3}$ of a set of 6 fish?

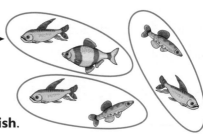

Split the fish into 3 equal groups.

Each group has 2 fish, so $\frac{1}{3}$ of 6 = 2.

$\frac{2}{3}$ is two groups, so $\frac{2}{3}$ of 6 fish = **4 fish**.

You can also divide, then multiply:

$\frac{1}{3}$ of 6 fish = 6 ÷ 3 = 2 fish

$\frac{2}{3}$ of 6 fish = 2 × 2 = **4 fish**

Set A

Copy out the eight dots for each question below.

Circle:

1. $\frac{3}{8}$ of the dots.

2. $\frac{2}{4}$ of the dots.

3. $\frac{3}{4}$ of the dots.

4. Mei has 16 fruits in a bowl. $\frac{3}{4}$ of the fruits are apples.

Complete the sentences below to find the number of apples in the bowl.

16 ÷ ☐ = ☐

☐ × 3 = ☐

So she has ☐ apples.

Find the missing numbers:

5. $\frac{1}{3}$ of 6 = ☐, so

$\frac{2}{3}$ of 6 = 2 × ☐ = ☐

6. $\frac{1}{4}$ of 8 = ☐, so

$\frac{3}{4}$ of 8 = 3 × ☐ = ☐

7. $\frac{1}{5}$ of 15 = ☐, so

$\frac{3}{5}$ of 15 = 3 × ☐ = ☐

Set B

Use the picture to help you answer the questions below.

What is:

1. $\frac{3}{4}$ of 12?

2. $\frac{4}{6}$ of 12?

Find the missing numbers:

3. one fifth of 25 = 5

two fifths of 25 = ☐

three fifths of 25 = ☐

4. one sixth of 36 = 6

four sixths of 36 = ☐

five sixths of 36 = ☐

What is:

5. $\frac{3}{4}$ of 4?

6. $\frac{2}{6}$ of 12?

7. $\frac{3}{10}$ of 20?

8. $\frac{4}{5}$ of 15?

9. $\frac{5}{8}$ of 32?

Set C

Work out:

1. $\frac{3}{5}$ of 45

2. $\frac{3}{8}$ of 40

3. $\frac{2}{4}$ of 60

4. two thirds of 12

5. three quarters of 20

Find the missing numbers:

6. $\frac{\square}{3}$ of 3 = 2

7. $\frac{\square}{4}$ of 12 = 9

8. $\frac{\square}{5}$ of 25 = 20

9. $\frac{\square}{10}$ of 50 = 30

10. Gilly thinks of a number. $\frac{2}{3}$ of her number is 6.

Which number is she thinking of?

11. Corey thinks of a number. $\frac{2}{5}$ of his number is 8.

Which number is he thinking of?

I can find non-unit fractions of an amount.

Solving Problems with Fractions

The skills you've learnt will help you solve the fraction problems on these next few pages.

Examples

Chloe has bought a new skateboard. $\frac{5}{6}$ is purple and the rest is pink.

What fraction of her skateboard is pink?

Draw a fraction bar with six equal parts:

$\frac{5}{6}$ of the skateboard is purple.

$\frac{6}{6} - \frac{5}{6} = \frac{1}{6}$, so this is the fraction of her skateboard that is pink.

Jeremy has fifteen animals on his farm. Three fifths of his animals are cows.

How many cows does he have?

Three fifths as a fraction is $\frac{3}{5}$.

Divide by the bottom number of the fraction: $15 \div 5 = 3$

Multiply by the top number of the fraction: $3 \times 3 = \mathbf{9\ cows}$

Set A

Heidi has these four pencils:

1   What fraction of her pencils are red?

Heidi buys another red pencil.

2   What fraction of her pencils are yellow?

Use the fraction bar to help you answer the questions below.

A loaf of bread is cut into 10 equal slices.

Gabby puts strawberry jam on five slices and raspberry jam on two slices.

What fraction of the slices:

3   have raspberry jam on?

4   have strawberry or raspberry jam on?

Gregor has 16 fish in his pond.

$\frac{1}{4}$ of his fish are orange and $\frac{2}{4}$ are white.

5   What fraction of his fish are orange or white?

6   How many fish are orange?

7   How many fish are white?

Vinnie has used $\frac{2}{5}$ of the pages in his diary.

8   What fraction of the diary has he not used?

His diary has 50 pages.

9   Complete the calculations below to work out how many pages of the diary he has used.

$50 \div 5 = \boxed{}$

$\boxed{} \times \boxed{} = \boxed{}$ pages

10   Tom buys 10 red pens and 10 blue pens.

He puts half of the red pens and a fifth of the blue pens in his bag.

How many pens are in his bag in total?

1. Cherie eats $\frac{1}{8}$ of an apple crumble in the afternoon and $\frac{2}{8}$ of it in the evening.

   What fraction of the apple crumble does she eat in total?

Einar has six guitars.

One third are electric guitars and the rest are acoustic.

2. What fraction of his guitars are acoustic?

3. How many acoustic guitars does he have?

A factory makes two sizes of model lorry:

- Model A: $\frac{1}{8}$ of the original lorry's length.

- Model B: $\frac{1}{10}$ of the original lorry's length.

4. Which model is longer?

The original lorry is 16 m long.

5. How many metres long is Model A?

Work out the missing numbers:

6. "One quarter of this number is 3."

7. "One fifth of this number is 10."

Amelie and Jamel are playing a game with counters.

Amelie is using grey counters.
Jamel is using blue counters.

There are four counters on a grid of nine squares:

How many more counters does:

8. Amelie need to add so one third of the squares are covered with grey counters?

9. Jamel need to add so two thirds of the squares are covered with blue counters?

An artist uses $\frac{1}{8}$ of a tin of paint to paint a picture.

There are 8 litres of paint in one tin.

1. How many pictures can she make with one whole tin of paint?

2. How many litres of paint does she use to paint a picture?

3. A bucket is full of water.
   One quarter of the water leaks from a hole in the bottom every minute.

   What fraction of the bucket has water in after two minutes?

Windy Mere is a lake that is 400 metres long.
Gusty Mere is one quarter of its length.
Breezy Mere is one half of its length.

4. Order the three lakes, from shortest to longest.

5. How long is Breezy Mere?

6. How long is Gusty Mere?

Dylan and Lucas share a bag of sweets:

- Dylan gets $\frac{1}{4}$ of the sweets.

- Lucas gets $\frac{1}{6}$ of the sweets.

7. Who has more sweets? Explain your answer.

Dylan shows the number of sweets he has below:

8. How many sweets were in the bag to start with?

Jack weighs the ingredients he needs to make a cupcake that weighs 60 grams.

The flour weighs $\frac{1}{5}$ as much as the cupcake.

The butter weighs $\frac{2}{5}$ as much as the cupcake.

9. What is the weight of the flour?

10. What is the total weight of the flour and the butter?

I can solve problems using fractions.

Fractions — Review 3

Copy and shade the final shape:

1 [diagram] + [diagram] = [diagram]

2 [diagram] + [diagram] = [diagram]

3 [diagram] + [diagram] = [diagram]

Work out:

4 $\frac{2}{4} + \frac{1}{4}$

5 $\frac{4}{6} + \frac{1}{6}$

6 $\frac{1}{3} + \frac{2}{3}$

7 $\frac{3}{8} + \frac{4}{8}$

8 $\frac{1}{9} + \frac{7}{9}$

9 $\frac{4}{10} + \frac{5}{10}$

Copy and shade the final shape:

10 [diagram] − [diagram] = [diagram]

11 [diagram] − [diagram] = [diagram]

12 [diagram] − [diagram] = [diagram]

Work out:

13 $\frac{3}{5} - \frac{2}{5}$

14 $\frac{4}{6} - \frac{3}{6}$

15 $\frac{7}{8} - \frac{2}{8}$

16 $\frac{3}{4} - \frac{3}{4}$

17 $\frac{7}{10} - \frac{4}{10}$

18 $\frac{9}{12} - \frac{7}{12}$

Find the missing values:

19 $\frac{7}{8} - \frac{\square}{8} = \frac{5}{8}$

20 $\frac{3}{5} + \frac{2}{\square} = 1$

21 $\frac{\square}{6} + \frac{1}{6} = \frac{5}{6}$

22 $1 - \frac{1}{4} = \frac{\square}{4}$

Use the picture below to help you find the missing numbers:

23 $\frac{1}{4}$ of 12 = $\square$

24 $\frac{1}{\square}$ of 12 = 4

What is:

25 $\frac{1}{2}$ of 4?

26 $\frac{1}{4}$ of 12?

27 $\frac{1}{5}$ of 20?

28 $\frac{1}{8}$ of 32?

29 $\frac{1}{2}$ of 42?

30 $\frac{1}{3}$ of 33?

Use the picture below to help you find the missing numbers:

31 $\frac{2}{5}$ of 15 = $\square$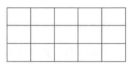

32 $\frac{\square}{5}$ of 15 = 12

What is:

33 $\frac{2}{3}$ of 9?

34 $\frac{2}{5}$ of 20?

35 $\frac{3}{4}$ of 12?

36 $\frac{6}{10}$ of 30?

37 $\frac{4}{5}$ of 50?

38 $\frac{5}{8}$ of 40?

Mathilde looks in her purse.
Two thirds of the coins are fifty pence coins.

39 What fraction of the coins are not fifty pence coins?

She counts twelve coins in her purse.

40 How many fifty pence coins does she have?

41 Seb plays the recorder for $\frac{1}{3}$ of his music lesson.

He plays the piano for twice as long as he plays the recorder.

What fraction of the lesson did he play the piano for?

A rabbit has ten carrots in his hutch.
He eats one fifth of the carrots a day.

42 How many carrots does he eat in one day?

43 What fraction of carrots has he eaten after the third day?

You must be a fraction genius after all of those questions!

Fractions — Challenges

1 There are four flowers in Flora's garden. Three of the flowers are shown below:

A   **B**   **C**

Three petals have fallen from Flower C.

a) What fraction of petals have <u>not</u> fallen from Flower C?

Flora describes the fourth flower:

"It has four sixths as many petals as Flower A and one half as many leaves as Flower B."

b) Draw the flower she has described.

2 Talat has a white rope, a blue rope and a red rope.
He cuts and throws away part of each rope.
He is left with:

- $\frac{1}{2}$ of the white rope

- $\frac{1}{3}$ of the blue rope

- $\frac{1}{4}$ of the red rope

All three of the remaining pieces are the same size.

Which rope was originally the longest? Explain your answer.

3 Look at the balance beam below.

A gymnast marks the beam with chalk to divide it into ten equal parts.
She then travels across the beam from left to right.

a) What fraction of the beam has she travelled?

b) How many fifths is this?

The balance beam is 5 m long.

c) Use your answer to part b) to work out how far she has travelled.

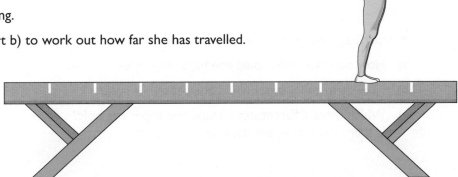

4   Chester digs for gemstones in the garden.

The table below shows how many gemstones he found each day.

Day	Gemstones found
Monday	12
Tuesday	10
Wednesday	8
Thursday	20

The gemstones he found were either purple or red.

*   On Monday and Tuesday, half of the gemstones he found were red.

*   On Wednesday and Thursday, one quarter of the gemstones he found were red.

How many purple gemstones did he find on:

a)   Monday?

b)   Tuesday?

c)   Wednesday?

d)   Thursday?

5   Four items in a shop are shown below.

Mug
$\frac{4}{10}$ kg

Book
$\frac{2}{10}$ kg

Teddy Bear
$\frac{3}{10}$ kg

Football
$\frac{5}{10}$ kg

A paper bag splits when it holds more than 1 kilogram of items.

a)   How many footballs could one paper bag hold?

b)   How many teddy bears could one paper bag hold?

c)   Which three different items could one paper bag hold?
     Is there more than one answer?

6 Look at the pattern of shapes on the right.

The next shape in the pattern is always twice as big as the shape before:

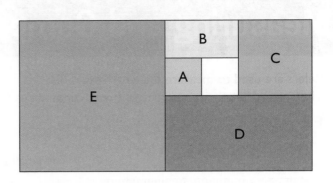

- Shape B is twice as big as Shape A.

- Shape C is twice as big as Shape B, and so on.

    True or false? Explain your answers.

    a) Shape B is $\frac{1}{2}$ as big as Shape C.

    b) $\frac{1}{8}$ of Shape E is the same size as Shape A.

    Shape D is half as big as Shape E.

    c) Write down two other facts about Shape D.

7 There are seven fractions in the cloud below.

Which two straight lines (A, B, C or D) would split the fractions into groups where the fractions in each group are all equal?

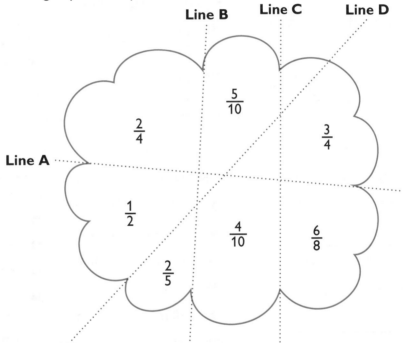

8 Travis the toucan only eats apples that show a fraction smaller than <u>one quarter</u>, and oranges that show a fraction larger than <u>one half</u>.

Which of the fruit below would Travis the toucan eat?

You've given your brain a good fraction workout after that — well done!

Measuring and Comparing Length

Rulers are used to measure the length of an object.
The units of length are millimetres (mm), centimetres (cm) and metres (m).

Example

Measure the length of this line.

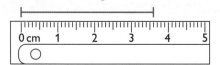

The small gaps on this ruler show 1 mm.

The length of the line is **3 cm 6 mm**.

You can also write this as **3.6 cm**.

Set A

What length is each arrow pointing to?

1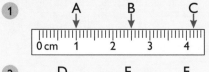

2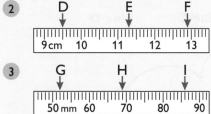

3

Draw a line that is:

4 6 cm long

5 80 mm long

Find the missing numbers:

6 1 m = ☐ cm

So 7 m = ☐ cm

7 1 cm = ☐ mm

So 5 cm = ☐ mm

Which is bigger:

8 6 cm or 6 m?

9 54 cm or 45 cm?

10 250 cm or 3 m?

Put these lengths in order, starting with the smallest:

11 56 m   56 cm   56 mm

12 4 m   350 cm   500 cm

Set B

Measure the length of these lines:

1

2

3

4

Find the missing numbers:

5 2 m = ☐ cm

6 8 cm = ☐ mm

7 26 cm = ☐ mm

8 90 mm = ☐ cm

9 170 mm = ☐ cm

10 5 m 20 cm = ☐ cm

Which symbol (< or >) should go in each box?

11 200 cm ☐ 3 m

12 640 mm ☐ 60 cm

13 8 m 54 cm ☐ 6 m 90 cm

14 Put these lengths in order, starting with the smallest:

8 m,   850 cm,   8 m 30 cm

Set C

Measure the longest side of these shapes:

1

2

3

4

Write these lengths in cm:

5 190 mm

6 15 m

7 $\frac{1}{2}$ m

8 9 m 84 cm

9 8 m 9 cm

10 10 m 60 cm

Which length is the longest:

11 200 cm or 20 m?

12 590 cm or 5 m 9 cm?

13 450 mm or 40 cm 6 mm?

14 A toy van is 9 cm long, a toy car is 85 mm long and a toy tractor is 8 cm 7 mm long. Put the toys in order of size, starting with the shortest.

I can measure and compare lengths.

Calculations with Length

Now it's time to use all those units of length in some calculations. Don't forget to put the units in your final answer.

Examples

Work out 52 cm + 30 cm.

52 + 30 = 82

So 52 cm + 30 cm = **82 cm**

Hardeep has a plastic pipe that is 1 m 93 cm long. He cuts off 48 cm. How much is left?

93 − 48 = 45

So he has **1 m 45 cm** of plastic pipe left.

Set A

Work out:

1. 72 cm + 20 cm
2. 140 mm − 30 mm
3. 700 mm + 200 mm
4. 195 m − 61 m
5. 44 mm + 38 mm
6. 82 cm − 39 cm
7. 1 m − 83 cm

Here are the lengths of 3 wires.

A: ⁓ 53 cm

B: ⁓ 26 cm

C: ⁓ 29 cm

8. What is the difference in length between wire A and wire B?

9. What is the total length of wire A and wire C?

10. Sophie's necklace is 43 cm. Her scarf is twice as long. How long is her scarf?

11. Karl walks 300 m then runs 420 m. How far has he gone in total?

12. A climber has a 54 m rope and cuts 19 m off. How much rope is left?

Set B

Find the missing numbers:

1. 35 mm + 59 mm = ⬜ mm
2. 178 m − ⬜ m = 118 m
3. ⬜ cm − 74 cm = 18 cm
4. 60 cm + 90 cm = 1 m ⬜ cm
5. 2 m ⬜ cm − 55 cm = 2 m
6. 1 m 40 cm − ⬜ cm = 90 cm

Here are the heights of 3 cakes.

Cake	A	B	C
Height (mm)	290	240	350

How much taller is:

7. cake A than cake B?
8. cake C than cake A?
9. What is the total height of all three cakes?

10. A tram travels 365 m to the first station. It then travels 480 m to the second station. How far does it travel in total?

Jill can swim 80 m. Raj can swim four times as far.

11. How far can Raj swim?
12. How far can Jill and Raj swim in total?

Set C

Work out:

1. 200 cm − 180 cm
2. 396 m + 9 m
3. 1 m − 50 cm
4. 11 cm 3 mm + 18 cm 6 mm
5. 4 m 51 cm + 2 m 22 cm
6. 6 cm 7 mm − 9 mm
7. 2 m − 1 m 40 cm

Work out the missing lengths on these ropes.

8.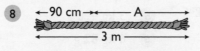
←90 cm→ ← A →
← 3 m →

9.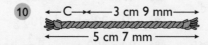
←56 cm→ ← 4 m 27 cm →
← B →

10.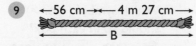
← C → ← 3 cm 9 mm →
← 5 cm 7 mm →

11. A school yard is 18 m long. The field is five times longer. How long is the field?

12. A house is 12 m 43 cm wide and gets extended by 1 m 40 cm. How wide is the extended house?

13. An apple tree is 5 m 40 cm tall. 80 cm is cut off the top. How tall is the tree now?

I can do calculations with lengths.

Measuring and Comparing Mass

The mass of an object tells you how heavy it is. The units of mass are grams (g) and kilograms (kg) — remember that there are 1000 g in 1 kg.

Examples

Find the mass of this piece of broccoli.

The small gaps on these scales show 50 g.

The mass of the broccoli is **550 g**.

Which mass is heavier, 5000 g or 7 kg?

5000 g = 5 kg ← There are 1000 g in 1 kg.

So **7 kg** is heavier.

Set A

1 How heavy are the boxes on these scales?

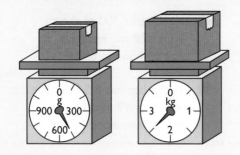

Copy this scale and draw an arrow at:

2 80 g

3 170 g

Find the missing numbers:

4 1 kg = ☐ g
So 6 kg = ☐ g

5 1000 g = ☐ kg
So 8000 g = ☐ kg

Which is heavier:

6 50 g or 50 kg?

7 600 g or 6 kg?

8 3000 g or 2 kg?

Put these masses in order, starting with the lightest:

9 | 255 g | 205 g | 250 g |

10 | 5 kg | 5400 g | 4800 g |

Set B

1 This scale shows how much Pedro weighs. How much does he weigh?

2 Mo weighs 65 kg. Tim weighs 80 kg. Copy the scale and draw arrows to show how much they weigh.

Write these in kg:

3 6000 g

4 9000 g

Write these in grams:

5 $\frac{1}{2}$ kg

6 1 kg 400 g

7 2 kg 700 g

Which mass is lighter:

8 4000 g or 5 kg?

9 8 kg 200 g or 8500 g?

10 3 kg 200 g or 3050 g?

11 Put these weights in order, starting with the heaviest:

Set C

Sasha weighs some ingredients. How much of each ingredient does she have?

1 cream cheese   2 caster sugar

3 She also has 140 g of biscuits and 155 g of butter. Put all four masses in order, starting with the heaviest.

Write these in grams:

4 $\frac{1}{4}$ kg

5 3 kg 420 g

6 6 kg 82 g

Which symbol (< or >) should go in each box?

7 4920 g ☐ 4 kg 800 g

8 3 kg 20 g ☐ 3100 g

9 9 kg 400 g ☐ $9\frac{1}{2}$ kg

10 Put these scales in order, starting with the scale showing the lightest weight.

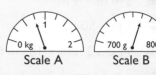

Scale A   Scale B

Scale C   Scale D

I can measure and compare mass.

Calculations with Mass

Adding and subtracting should be nothing new — the only difference here is they're units of mass.
Careful though, you can't just add or subtract two units if one is in kilograms and the other is in grams.

Examples

Work out 450 g – 300 g.

450 – 300 = 150

So 450 g – 300 g = **150 g**

Isobel's rabbit eats 200 g of carrots.
Her horse eats 8 kg 500 g of carrots.
What mass of carrots do her animals eat in total?

500 + 200 = 700

So in total they eat **8 kg 700 g** of carrots.

Set A

Work out:

1. 64 g + 30 g
2. 190 g – 60 g
3. 600 kg + 300 kg
4. 420 g – 200 g
5. 200 g – 40 g
6. 2 kg + 400 g
7. 1 kg – 300 g

Look at the two scales below.

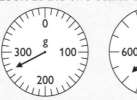

8. What is the difference in mass between the two scales?
9. What is the total mass shown on the two scales?

Ian buys 40 g of tomatoes. How much does Mike buy if he:

10. gets twice as much as Ian?
11. gets 5 times as much as Ian?

A sweetshop has 4 kg of jelly snakes. What mass of jelly snakes do they have if they:

12. buy 600 g more?
13. sell 700 g?

Set B

Work out:

1. 250 g + 270 g
2. 450 kg + 69 kg
3. 1 kg + 500 g
4. 9 kg – 800 g
5. 3 kg 100 g + 700 g
6. 5 kg 800 g – 300 g
7. 14 kg 400 g – 6 kg 100 g

Look at these boxes.

How much heavier is:

8. box A than box C?
9. box B than box A?
10. What is the total weight of all three boxes?

11. A leopard weighs 52 kg. A gorilla weighs three times as much. How much does the gorilla weigh?

Sam's toy train is 1 kg 200 g and each carriage is 300 g. What is the total mass of:

12. the train and one carriage?
13. the train and two carriages?

Set C

Work out:

1. 380 g + 560 g
2. 405 kg – 90 kg
3. 7 kg – 400 g
4. 5 kg 200 g + 600 g
5. 8 kg 400 g + 2 kg 500 g
6. 5 kg 200 g – 300 g
7. 9 kg 100 g – 3 kg 200 g

Here are the masses of 3 rabbits.

Waffles	2 kg 100 g
Murphy	1 kg 500 g
Daisy	800 g

8. What is the total mass of Waffles and Daisy?

Find the difference in the masses of:

9. Murphy and Daisy.
10. Waffles and Murphy.

11. What mass is four times as heavy as 32 g?

Imran and Joan go blackberry picking. Imran picks 3 kg 250 g and Joan picks 1 kg 650 g.

12. How much do they pick in total?
13. How much more does Imran pick than Joan?

I can do calculations with mass.

Measuring and Comparing Capacity

Capacity tells you the amount that something can hold. The units of capacity are millilitres (ml) and litres (l).

Examples

How much water is in this beaker?

The small gaps are 10 ml.

So there is **30 ml** of water.

Which is bigger, $7\frac{1}{2}$ litres or 7 litres 600 ml?

$7\frac{1}{2}$ litres = 7 litres 500 ml.

So **7 litres 600 ml** is bigger.

Set A

1. How much water is in each of these beakers?

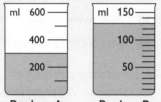

Beaker A   Beaker B

2. Which beaker has more water in it?

Find the missing numbers:

3. 1 litre = ☐ ml
   So 4 litres = ☐ ml

4. 1000 ml = ☐ litres
   So 9000 ml = ☐ litres

Which is bigger:

5. 8 ml or 8 litres?

6. 500 ml or 5 litres?

Put these amounts in order, starting with the smallest:

7. | 320 ml   330 ml   300 ml |

8. | 5 litres   4 litres   3000 ml |

Put these amounts in order, starting with the biggest:

9. | 80 ml   800 ml   8 litres |

10. | 150 ml   1500 ml   1 litre |

Set B

Look at these bottles of juice.

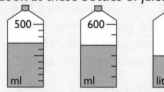

Bottle A   Bottle B   Bottle C

Which bottle contains more juice:

1. Bottle A or Bottle B?

2. Bottle B or Bottle C?

Write these amounts in ml:

3. 8 litres

4. 6 litres 200 ml

5. 7 litres 800 ml

Which amount is smaller:

6. 5 litres or 650 ml?

7. 2 litres 500 ml or 2800 ml?

Are these true or false?

8. 1 litre 300 ml = 1300 ml

9. $4\frac{1}{2}$ litres = 4 litres 50 ml

10. Put these amounts in order, starting with the smallest:

3 litres 200 ml	3800 ml
3 litres 600 ml	$3\frac{1}{2}$ litres

Set C

1. How much water is in each of the measuring cylinders below?

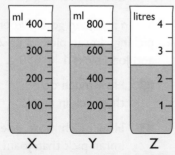

X   Y   Z

Write these in millilitres:

2. $\frac{1}{10}$ litre

3. 4 litres 790 ml

4. 9 litres 74 ml

Which amount is bigger:

5. 4 litres 800 ml or 4900 ml?

6. 3 litres 50 ml or 3400 ml?

7. 8 litres 600 ml or $8\frac{1}{2}$ litres?

8. Put these bottles in order, starting with the bottle containing the most water:

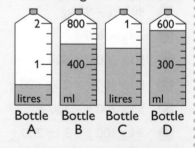

Bottle A   Bottle B   Bottle C   Bottle D

I can measure and compare capacity.

Calculations with Capacity

You've measured and compared capacity, now for some calculations. Remember to pay attention to the units.

Examples

Work out 320 ml + 200 ml

    320 + 200 = 520

    So 320 ml + 200 ml = **520 ml**

Fred has 1 litre 800 ml of lemonade in a bottle.
He pours out 700 ml. How much is left in the bottle?

800 − 700 = 100

So there is **1 litre 100 ml** of lemonade left.

Set A

Work out:

1. 41 ml + 50 ml
2. 340 litres − 20 litres
3. 400 ml + 400 ml
4. 680 litres − 200 litres
5. 400 ml − 80 ml
6. 1 litre + 750 ml
7. 3 litres − 400 ml

Look at this beaker of water.

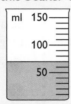

8. How much more water is needed to fill it to 150 ml?
9. How much will be left if 39 ml is poured out?

A bottle of perfume can hold 80 ml. What is the capacity of:

10. two bottles?
11. five bottles?

A bath can hold 300 litres.
A hot tub can hold 650 litres.

12. How much more can the hot tub hold than the bath?
13. What is the total capacity?

Set B

Work out:

1. 210 ml + 300 ml
2. 250 litres − 38 litres
3. 2 litres + 500 ml
4. 5 litres − 100 ml
5. 2 litres 200 ml + 600 ml
6. 4 litres 420 ml − 200 ml
7. 9 litres 500 ml − 6 litres

The capacities are written on the sides of these buckets.

8. How much more can the red bucket hold than the orange bucket?
9. What is the total capacity of the red and blue buckets?

10. What capacity is three times as much as 45 ml?
11. A bottle of orange juice holds 1 litre 500 ml. Ellen drinks 300 ml. How much juice is left in the bottle?
12. Hans has 2 litres 400 ml of red paint and 500 ml of blue paint. How much paint does he have in total?

Set C

Work out:

1. 490 ml + 180 ml
2. 675 litres + 50 litres
3. 5 litres − 600 ml
4. 1 litre 300 ml + 2 litres 600 ml
5. 4 litres 600 ml − 900 ml
6. 7 litres 500 ml − 600 ml
7. 4 litres 200 ml − 1 litre 300 ml

8. A small yoghurt pot has a capacity of 65 ml. What is the total capacity of four small yoghurt pots?

Sumi has this bottle of strawberry milk.

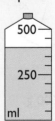

9. How much more does she need to have 2 litres of strawberry milk?

Here is a recipe for fruit punch.

> 300 ml soda water
> 1 litre 100 ml apple juice
> 1 litre 400 ml lemonade

10. How much more lemonade is needed than soda water?
11. How much less soda water is needed than apple juice?
12. How much fruit punch will the recipe make?

I can do calculations with capacity.

Measurement — Review 1

Measure the length of these lines:

1

2

3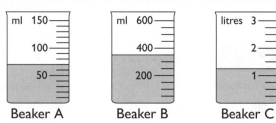

Find the missing numbers:

4 3 m = ☐ cm

7 50 mm = ☐ cm

5 7 cm = ☐ mm

8 200 cm = ☐ m

6 15 cm = ☐ mm

9 140 mm = ☐ cm

Put these lengths in order, starting with the shortest:

10 48 m, 48 cm, 5 m

11 6 m, 550 cm, 5 m 8 cm

12 63 mm, 6 cm 8 mm, 7 cm, 69 mm

Work out:

13 43 cm + 56 cm

16 400 m – 60 m

14 250 m – 40 m

17 3 m 62 cm + 28 cm

15 164 m + 500 m

18 5 cm 6 mm – 7 mm

Harry did the long jump at sports day. His first jump was 2 m and his second jump was 3 m 40 cm.

19 What was the difference between his two jumps?

20 What was the total distance of his two jumps?

Work out the weight shown on each of these scales:

21

23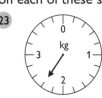

22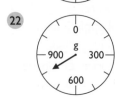

24

Write these in grams:

25 3 kg

27 1 kg 600 g

26 $\frac{1}{5}$ kg

28 5 kg 850 g

Which mass is lighter:

29 200 g or 3 kg?

31 5 kg 300 g or 5400 g?

30 8500 g or 8 kg?

32 4 kg 100 g or 4050 g?

Work out:

33 380 g – 20 g

36 5 kg – 300 g

34 160 g + 600 g

37 7 kg 200 g + 700 g

35 1 kg + 400 g

38 3 kg 400 g – 800 g

Small bags of potatoes weigh 400 g.
Large bags weigh 2 kg 300 g. How much do:

39 two small bags weigh in total?

40 a small and a large bag weigh in total?

41 How much heavier is a large bag than a small bag?

42 How much water is inside each of these beakers?

ml 150	ml 600	litres 3
100	400	2
50	200	1
Beaker A	Beaker B	Beaker C

Write these amounts in ml:

43 2 litres

45 3 litres 100 ml

44 6 litres

46 8 litres 75 ml

Put these capacities in order, starting with the biggest:

47 790 ml, 799 ml, 709 ml

48 2 litres 50 ml, 2500 ml, 2 litres 800 ml

49 $\frac{1}{2}$ litre, 650 ml, 2 litres, 520 ml

Work out:

50 580 ml – 60 ml

53 3 litres – 600 ml

51 870 ml – 500 ml

54 4 litres 300 ml + 500 ml

52 2 litres + 700 ml

55 9 litres 500 ml – 900 ml

56 Wes has a watering can with 5 litres of water in it. After watering the flowers, there is 2 litres 400 ml of water left. How much water did he use?

Wow, you've definitely got the measure of those questions — well done!

Perimeter

The perimeter is the distance all the way around the outside of a 2D shape. To find it, you just add up the lengths of every side of the shape — sometimes you'll have to measure them first.

Examples

Work out the perimeter of this triangle.

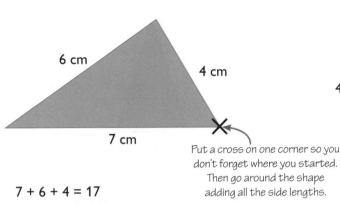

7 + 6 + 4 = 17

So the triangle's perimeter is **17 cm**.

Put a cross on one corner so you don't forget where you started. Then go around the shape adding all the side lengths.

Measure the perimeter of the shape below.

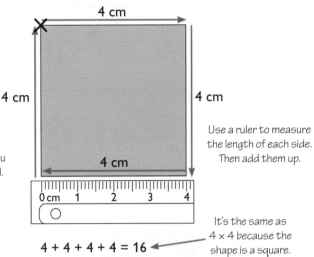

Use a ruler to measure the length of each side. Then add them up.

4 + 4 + 4 + 4 = 16

It's the same as 4 × 4 because the shape is a square.

So the shape's **perimeter is 16 cm**.

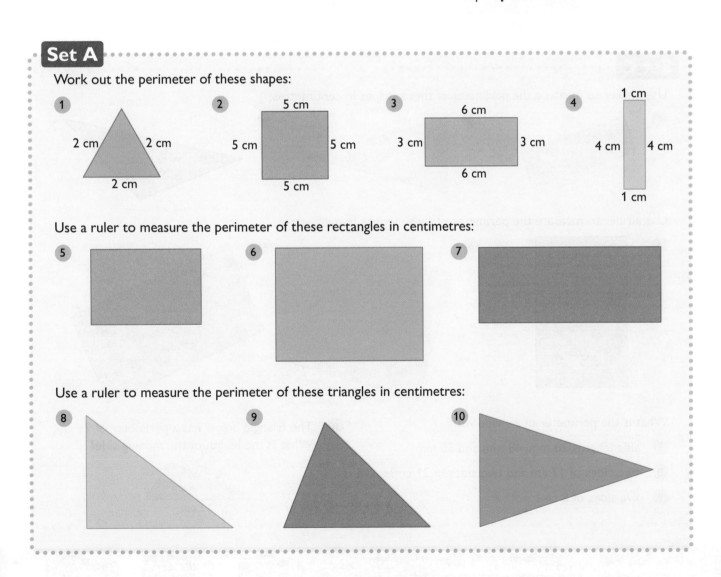

Set A

Work out the perimeter of these shapes:

1. (triangle: 2 cm, 2 cm, 2 cm)
2. (square: 5 cm, 5 cm, 5 cm, 5 cm)
3. (rectangle: 6 cm, 3 cm, 6 cm, 3 cm)
4. (rectangle: 1 cm, 4 cm, 1 cm, 4 cm)

Use a ruler to measure the perimeter of these rectangles in centimetres:

5.
6.
7.

Use a ruler to measure the perimeter of these triangles in centimetres:

8.
9.
10.

Use a ruler to measure the perimeter of these shapes in centimetres:

1

2

3

Use a ruler to measure the perimeter of these shapes in millimetres:

4

5

6

7 Work out the perimeter of this screen.

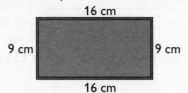

16 cm
9 cm   9 cm
16 cm

What is the perimeter of a shape with:

8 side lengths 7 cm, 5 cm and 4 cm?

9 side lengths 10 cm, 8 cm, 10 cm and 8 cm?

10 four 6 cm sides?

Use a ruler to measure the perimeter of these shapes in centimetres:

1

2

3

Use a ruler to measure the perimeter of these shapes in millimetres:

4

5

6

What is the perimeter of a shape with:

7 side lengths 20 mm, 48 mm and 35 mm?

8 two sides of 17 cm and two sides of 21 cm?

9 five sides of 8 cm?

10 The triangle below has a perimeter of 26 cm. What is the length of the missing side?

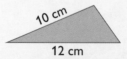

10 cm

12 cm

I can measure the perimeter of shapes.

  ✓ ✓   ✓

Calculations with Money — 1

Money can be given in pounds (£) and pence (p). You'll often see amounts like £5 and 20p written as £5.20, but it means the same thing. The bit before the decimal point is the pounds and the bit after is the pence.

Examples

Work out £2.30 + 60p.

£2.30 = 230p
230 + 60 = 290
So £2.30 + 60p = 290p or **£2.90**

Anika spent £5.50 on a skirt and £1.20 on a tennis ball. How much did she spend in total?

£5.50 = 550p and £1.20 = 120p
550 + 120 = 670
So Anika spent 670p or **£6.70**.

Set A

Work out:

1. 43p + 54p
2. £150 + £40
3. £300 + £500
4. £3 + 80p
5. £9 + 20p
6. £10 + 60p
7. £21 + £8 + 40p

Find the missing numbers:

8. £4.50 = ☐ p
9. 190p = £ ☐

Bob has these coins in his pocket.

 × 2   × 7   × 8

How much does he have:

10. in pounds and pence?
11. in pence?

How much does each person spend?

12. Adam buys a TV for £250 and a TV stand for £45.
13. Lucy buys two newspapers for 38p each.
14. Cara buys a sandwich for £3 and crisps for 65p.
15. Tamal buys two packs of stickers for 40p each and a sticker book for £5.

Set B

Work out:

1. £300 + £180
2. £7 + 80p
3. £15 + 35p
4. £4.30 + £3
5. £7.60 + £6
6. £1.30 + 60p
7. £7.10 + 45p

Work out how to make:

8. £1.30 using 3 coins
9. £1.08 using 4 coins
10. £1.61 using 4 coins
11. £3.75 using 5 coins

12. Sinead has £4.40 and her sister has 55p. How much do they have in total?

Here is a price list for some fruit.

Pear 35p   Grapes £2.10
Apple 40p   Melon £1.50

How much would it cost to buy:

13. five apples?
14. a pear and a melon?
15. two apples and a pack of grapes?

Set C

Work out:

1. £1.25 + 40p
2. £4.33 + 18p
3. £3.50 + 90p
4. £6.40 + 70p
5. £7.30 + 50p + 70p
6. £1.40 + £2.50
7. £3.40 + £5.70

8. Andy spent £4.20 on a cinema ticket and £3.50 on popcorn. How much did he spend in total?

Ice lollies cost 80p each and ice creams cost £1.40 each. How much would it cost to buy:

9. an ice lolly and an ice cream?
10. four ice lollies?
11. two ice creams?

Becca buys a pen for £2.50 and a pencil for 65p.

12. How much does she pay altogether?
13. Which 4 coins could she use to pay the exact amount?

14. Zak paid £2.30 for a bus ticket and £5.80 for a train ticket. How much did he pay in total?

I can add amounts of money.

Calculations with Money — 2

More money calculation questions coming right up — this time it's all about finding the amount of money left or the amount of change.

Examples

Work out £4.80 – 70p.

    £4.80 = 480p
    480 – 70 = 410
    So £4.80 – 70p = 410p or **£4.10**

Michael buys a chocolate bar for 82p.
He pays with a £2 coin.
How much change does Michael get?

By counting up:

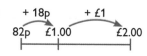

£1 + 18p = **£1.18**

Set A

Work out:

1. 87p – 54p
2. £180 – £30
3. £900 – £400
4. £1 – 30p
5. £3 – 50p
6. £7 – 20p
7. £9 – 60p

8. Kim has 43p and wants to buy a badge for 78p. How much more money does she need?

9. Will had £400 and spent £90 on a bike. How much does he have left?

10. Spencer paid £270 for a games console and a game. The game was £50. How much was the games console?

Here are some prices in a butcher's shop.

> Sausages 60p
> Meatballs 40p

How much change would you get from £1 if you bought:

11. one sausage?

12. two meatballs?

13. How much change would you get from £5 if you bought one sausage and one meatball?

Set B

Work out:

1. £450 – £110
2. £1 – 65p
3. £5 – 70p
4. £3.90 – £2
5. £8.65 – 60p
6. £5 – £2.70
7. £10 – £6.90

8. Una buys a lolly for 30p and some bubble gum for 25p. How much change does she get from £1?

Blaise has £5. How much change would he get after buying:

9. a football for £3.50?

10. a book for £2.90?

11. two rubbers for 45p each?

Look at this price list.

| pencil 65p | fountain pen £2.30 |
| ruler £1.10 | calculator £5.50 |

How much cheaper is:

12. a pencil than a ruler?

13. a ruler than a calculator?

14. How much change would you get from £10 if you bought two fountain pens?

Set C

Work out:

1. £2 – 40p
2. £5.62 – 16p
3. £2.20 – 30p
4. £5 – £1.30
5. £9 – £3.30
6. £10 – £2.70
7. £7.30 – £2.10

8. Felix has £1 and buys eight sweets for 7p each. How much change does he get?

9. Dan has £9.50. How much more money would he need to buy a backpack for £14.90?

10. Jill has £5. She buys a box of cereal for £1.80 and some milk for 60p. How much does she have left?

Look at the gifts below.

£2.85   £4.75   £3.40
Gift A   Gift B   Gift C

How much cheaper is:

11. gift C than gift B?

12. gift A than gift C?

13. How much change will you get if you buy gifts A and B with £10?

I can subtract amounts of money and find change.

Measurement — Review 2

Work out the perimeter of these shapes:

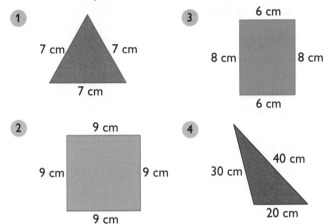

① 7 cm 7 cm 7 cm

③ 6 cm 8 cm 8 cm 6 cm

② 9 cm 9 cm 9 cm 9 cm

④ 40 cm 30 cm 20 cm

Use a ruler to measure the perimeter of these shapes in millimetres:

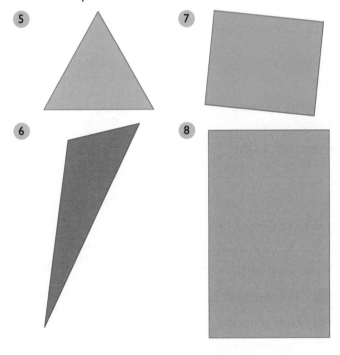

⑤

⑦

⑥

⑧

What is the perimeter of a shape with:

⑨ four sides of 10 cm?

⑩ side lengths 8 cm, 9 cm and 15 cm?

⑪ two sides of 9 cm and two sides of 12 cm?

⑫ The perimeter of this triangle is 32 cm. What is the length of the missing side?

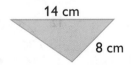

14 cm

8 cm

Work out:

⑬ £280 + £300

⑭ £5 + 40p

⑮ £7 + 59p

⑯ £2.50 + £4

⑰ £9.30 + 20p

⑱ £2.80 + 50p

⑲ £4.60 + £3.30

⑳ £4.20 + £3.90

In pounds and pence, what are the totals of these coins?

㉑ £2 × 3   20p × 2   1p × 4

㉒ £1 × 3   50p × 1   20p × 1   2p × 2

㉓ Glasses cost £120 and sunglasses cost £59. How much does it cost to buy both?

㉔ Nigel spends £2.10 on a fruit salad and 65p on a doughnut. How much does he spend in total?

㉕ At the local shop tins of beans cost 60p. How much does it cost to buy five tins of beans?

Work out:

㉖ £630 – £200

㉗ 85p – 68p

㉘ £1 – 40p

㉙ £5.50 – £3

㉚ £7.35 – 20p

㉛ £5 – £3.95

㉜ £10 – £7.10

㉝ £5.90 – £3.20

Here are some prices of drinks at a cafe. How much cheaper is:

cola   £1.75
water   80p
tea   £1.85
coffee   £2.50

㉞ water than tea?

㉟ water than cola?

㊱ tea than coffee?

How much change would you get if you bought:

㊲ one tea using a £5 note?

㊳ one coffee using a £10 note?

㊴ two waters using a £5 note?

㊵ Joanna has £6.80 in her pocket. She accidentally drops £1.90. How much is left in her pocket?

Well done for tackling all those perimeter and money questions — you're a superstar!

Telling the Time — 1

Telling the time can be tricky, but it comes in handy every day. So you'll need to concentrate here and make sure you can read any analogue clock — even ones with Roman numerals.

Examples

Write the time shown on the clock in words.

The long hand is pointing to the 25th minute.
The short hand has gone past 6.

So the time is **twenty-five past six**.

Draw the hands on a clock to show that it is thirteen minutes to twelve.

The short hand needs to point between **11 and 12** (closer to 12).

The long hand needs to point to the **47th** minute (60 − 13 = 47).

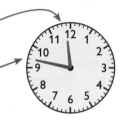

What time does this clock show?

The long hand is pointing to quarter past the hour.

The short hand is pointing just past VIII, which is 8 in Roman numerals.

So the time is **quarter past eight**.

Some clocks use Roman numerals instead of numbers. Here is what they all mean:

I = 1	VII = 7
II = 2	VIII = 8
III = 3	IX = 9
IV = 4	X = 10
V = 5	XI = 11
VI = 6	XII = 12

Set A

Look at the clocks below.

A

B

C

D

On a copy of the clock on the right, draw hands to show:

5 Ten past five

6 Nine o'clock

7 Twenty to two

8 Twenty-seven minutes past eleven

Write the times shown below in words:

9

11

10

12

Write the letter of the clock that shows:

1 Twelve o'clock

2 Half past two

3 Quarter past nine

4 Seven minutes to five

Set B

Write the times shown below in words:

①

③

②

④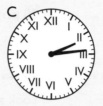

On a copy of the clock on the right, draw hands to show:

⑤ Nine o'clock

⑥ Quarter to six

⑦ Twenty past eight

⑧ Ten past twelve

⑨ Twenty-five past seven

Look at the clocks below:

A

B

C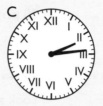

D

Write the letter of the clock that shows:

⑩ 14 minutes past 2

⑪ 9 minutes to 12

⑫ 27 minutes past 1

⑬ 22 minutes to 10

⑭ What time was it 30 minutes after noon? Give your answer in words.

Set C

Write the times shown below in words:

①

④

②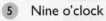

⑤

③

⑥

⑦ What time will it be 60 minutes after midnight? Give your answer in words.

⑧ What time was it 52 minutes before noon? Give your answer in words.

⑨ What time will this clock show 37 minutes later? Give your answer in words.

⑩ What time did this clock show 18 minutes earlier? Give your answer in words.

⑪ What time will this clock show 2 hours and 55 minutes later? Give your answer in words.

I can tell and write the time from analogue clocks.

Telling the Time — 2

Digital clocks give you the time in numbers — you can have 12-hour or 24-hour digital clocks.
For 12-hour clocks, you need to remember that "am" means morning, and "pm" means afternoon and evening.

Examples

Write these times using the 12-hour clock.

- Quarter past eight in the morning **8:15 am**

- Ten to five in the afternoon **4:50 pm**

Write the time shown on the clock in words.
Is the time before or after noon?

The time is **twenty-five past four**. It is after **noon**.

Set A

Look at the clocks below.

A `6:30 AM`   B `1:55 PM`

C `10:15 PM`   D `2:05 AM`

Which clock shows:

1. quarter past ten?

2. half past six?

3. a time in the afternoon?

Look at these 24-hour clocks.

E `09:10`   F `00:00`

G `21:10`   H `12:00`

Which clock shows:

4. noon?

5. midnight?

6. ten past nine in the morning?

Write the times shown on these clocks in words.

7. `06:30`

8. `15:00`

9. `09:55`

10. `20:10`

Set B

Write the times on these clocks in words. Say if the time is before or after noon.

1. `11:25`   4. `08:50`

2. `16:00`   5. `10:18`

3. `05:45`   6. `19:26`

Write these times using the 12-hour clock:

7. half past nine in the morning

8. twenty-five past three in the afternoon

9. quarter to seven in the evening

10. five to four in the morning

11. twenty past midnight

Write these times using the 24-hour clock:

12. half past eight in the morning

13. ten minutes to noon

14. quarter past nine in the evening

15. twenty to three in the afternoon

Set C

Write the times shown below in words. Say if the time is before noon or after noon.

1. `11:50`   4. `10:48`

2. `00:30`   5. `22:11`

3. `17:45`   6. `20:53`

Write these times using both the 12-hour and 24-hour clocks:

7. half past one in the afternoon

8. twenty-five to eleven in the morning

9. five minutes to midnight

10. ten to seven in the morning

11. twelve minutes past eight in the evening

Use the 24-hour clock to write the time that is:

12. 18 minutes before 14:00

13. 37 minutes after 07:30

14. 50 minutes after 17:45

15. 21 minutes before noon

16. 4 hours 19 minutes after 23:30

I can tell and write the time from digital clocks.

Months and Years

Once you know how many days are in a year, a leap year is easy — it's only one day longer with 366 days. The months are trickier — you just have to learn how many days each has.

Example

Grant's birthday is on 28th August.
Oliver's birthday is 5 days later.

When is Oliver's birthday?

Count up the days:

Oliver's birthday is on **2nd September**.

Set A

Pick the number from the box that shows the number of days in:

30	
	366
31	
	365
28	

1. October
2. a normal year
3. February in a normal year
4. April
5. a leap year

What date is:

6. 1 day after 30th September?
7. 1 day before 1st August?
8. Azi's birthday is on 30th March. John's birthday is 2 days later. When is John's birthday?
9. Ivan's birthday is on 1st July. Sally's birthday is 3 days earlier. When is Sally's birthday?

10. How many days does February have in a leap year?
11. Jeremy goes to school on 20 days in November. How many days in November does he <u>not</u> go to school?
12. Caley eats corn flakes on 11 days in May. How many days in May does she <u>not</u> eat corn flakes?

Set B

How many days are there in:

1. a normal year?
2. September?
3. a leap year?
4. July?
5. May?
6. February in a leap year?
7. December?

8. Jay's birthday is on 28th June. Fred's is 1 week later. When is Fred's birthday?
9. Ian drinks tea on 16 days in February. It is not a leap year. How many days in February does he not drink tea?
10. Ira's birthday is on 10th April. Raj's birthday is 12 days earlier. When is Raj's birthday?

11. Tim starts school on 29th August. Betty starts school on 2nd September. How many days after Tim starts does Betty start?
12. What date is two weeks after 20th January?
13. It is sunny on half the days in April. On how many days in April is it sunny?

Set C

1. In a leap year, how many more days are in August than February?

How many days are there in:

2. spring (March, April, May)?
3. autumn (September, October, November)?
4. two leap years?
5. the first three months of a normal year?

6. What date is 1 week after 23rd February, in a leap year?
7. What date is 15 days before 9th July?
8. Lee's birthday is on 4th January. Kalid's is 2 weeks earlier. When is Kalid's birthday?
9. 2012 was a leap year. How many days were there in 2012 and 2013 altogether?

10. Asha has her hair cut on 25th July. Tom has his cut on 5th August. How many days before Tom does Asha have her hair cut?
11. Caris eats an orange on a quarter of the days in February. It is not a leap year. On how many days in February does Caris eat an orange?

I know the number of days in each month, year and leap year.

Seconds, Minutes and Hours

60 seconds in one minute. 60 minutes in one hour. Just remember 60 and you'll be sorted.

Examples

How much longer is 1 min than 28 secs?

1 minute = 60 seconds
60 − 28 = 32
So it is **32 seconds** longer.

Amid took 14 mins 30 secs to finish his homework and Livvy took 14 mins 10 secs. Who was fastest?

The minutes are the same for both.
30 secs is longer than 10 secs.
So **Livvy** was fastest.

Set A

Find the shortest time in each list.

1. 24 secs, 42 secs, 23 secs
2. 402 mins, 412 mins, 420 mins
3. 20 mins, 20 hrs, 20 secs
4. 1 hr 5 mins, 1 hr 48 mins, 1 hr 13 mins
5. 1 min 54 secs, 55 secs, 1 min
6. 1 hr 56 mins, 2 hrs, 2 hrs 12 mins

Work out:

7. 52 secs − 18 secs
8. 41 mins − 29 mins
9. 1 min − 34 secs

How much longer is:

10. 49 secs than 12 secs?
11. 1 min than 17 secs?
12. 3 mins 20 secs than 10 secs?

Look at these running race times:

Name	Time
Ben	2 mins 35 secs
Nevin	1 min 42 secs
Leah	1 min 59 secs

13. Who was the fastest?
14. Who was the slowest?
15. How many seconds did Nevin run for in total?

Set B

Find the longest time in each list.

1. 52 secs, 54 secs, 45 secs
2. 23 mins, 5 hours, 45 secs
3. 1 min 2 secs, 55 secs, 2 mins
4. Put these four times in order, starting with the shortest:

4 hrs 24 mins	4 hrs 48 mins
4 hrs 42 mins	4 hrs 40 mins

How much longer is:

5. 1 min than 41 secs?
6. 4 hrs 30 mins than 22 mins?
7. 3 mins 10 secs than 50 secs?
8. 7 hrs 45 mins than 2 hrs?
9. Jack took 10 mins 50 secs to finish a puzzle and Maggie took 8 mins 20 secs. How much quicker was Maggie?

Look at these rowing race times:

Name	Time
Zoe	15 mins 46 secs
Farid	16 mins 10 secs
Melissa	15 mins 40 secs

10. Who was the second fastest?
11. Salma took 1 minute 20 seconds less than Farid. How long did she take?

Set C

How much longer is:

1. 1 min than 39 secs?
2. 3 mins than 21 secs?
3. 9 hrs than 6 hrs 20 mins?
4. 2 mins 40 secs than 50 secs?
5. 8 hrs 40 mins than 4 hrs 20 mins?
6. 9 mins 10 secs than 6 mins 40 secs?

Look at these marathon times:

Name	Time
Priya	4 hrs 55 mins 50 secs
Hayley	5 hrs 16 mins 12 secs
Ned	5 hrs 4 mins 20 secs
Ryu	5 hrs 12 mins 50 secs

7. Who was the slowest?
8. Who was the fastest?
9. How much slower was Ned than Priya?

It took Lee 9 mins 46 secs to answer a tricky maths problem.

10. Liz did it 2 mins 1 sec quicker than Lee. How long did she take?
11. Mo took 10 mins 15 secs. How much slower was he than Lee?
12. Jan took 8 mins 50 secs. How much quicker was she than Lee?

I can compare times in seconds, minutes and hours.

Time Problems

These questions cover things like working out how long something takes, or when something starts or finishes.

Examples

Kyle starts watching a film at 4:50 pm. It finishes at 6:15 pm. How long is the film?

Count on in steps from 4:50 pm:

So the length of the film is:
10 mins + 1 hour + 15 mins = **1 hour 25 minutes**

A concert lasted 2 hours 20 minutes. It ended at 16:25. What time did the concert start? Give your answer using the 24-hour clock.

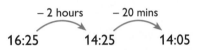

So the concert started at **14:05**.

The table below shows the times of two cooking classes.

Class	Time
Pizza	10:30 am – 11:50 am
Pastry	1:15 pm – 2:45 pm

Which class is longer?

Pizza class is 30 mins + 50 mins = 80 mins long

```
    + 45 mins       + 45 mins
1:15 pm     2:00 pm        2:45 pm
```

Pastry class is 45 mins + 45 mins = 90 mins long

So **pastry class** is longer.

Set A

1. Hannah started reading at 4 pm and finished at 7 pm. How long did she read for?

2. Dance club starts at 5:00 pm. It lasts 1 hour 30 minutes. What time does it finish? Give your answer in words.

3. Story time lasts for 30 minutes. It finishes at 3:35 pm. When does story time start? Give your answer using the 12-hour clock.

4. Mina starts climbing a hill at 10:15. She reaches the top of the hill at 12:45. How long does it take her to get to the top?

5. Clare did a jigsaw one evening. These clocks show when she started and finished.

start   finish

How long did it take her to do the jigsaw?

Look at the fair timetable below.

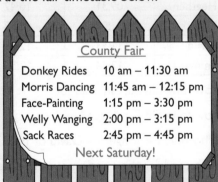

County Fair

Donkey Rides	10 am – 11:30 am
Morris Dancing	11:45 am – 12:15 pm
Face-Painting	1:15 pm – 3:30 pm
Welly Wanging	2:00 pm – 3:15 pm
Sack Races	2:45 pm – 4:45 pm

Next Saturday!

6. How long are the donkey rides on for?

7. How long does the Morris dancing last?

8. Which is on for longer — welly wanging or the sack races?

9. Ged starts swimming at 17:00 and finishes at 18:20. How long does he swim for?

10. Lenny starts playing football at 12:10. He plays for 1 hour 30 minutes. When does he finish playing? Give your answer using the 24-hour clock.

Set B

1. Daisy sets off on a walk at 4 pm.
   She gets back home at 6:15 pm.
   How long does Daisy walk for?

2. The school day starts at 09:00. It lasts for
   six and a half hours. When does the school
   day end? Give your answer in words.

3. Lunchtime lasts for 1 hour 15 minutes.
   It finishes at 13:25. What time does it start?
   Give your answer using the 12-hour clock.

Part of the TV guide
for Channel One is
shown on the right.

| 18:10 — The Run |
| 18:45 — News |
| 19:35 — Lord of the Pies |
| 20:20 — Dig, Dog, Dig! |

4. Laurie turns on Channel One at 18:20.
   How long is it until the next show starts?

5. How long is "Lord of the Pies" on for?

6. The News is shown on Channel Two
   1 hour 10 minutes before Channel One.
   What time is the News shown on Channel Two?
   Give your answer using the 24-hour clock.

The table shows the times of some
bus journeys from London.

DESTINATION	LEAVES	ARRIVES
York	06:45	11:50
Birmingham	09:15	12:35
Liverpool	11:20	16:45
Exeter	14:15	18:10
Cardiff	19:30	22:55

7. How long is the journey to Birmingham?

8. How long is the journey to Cardiff?

9. Which is longer — the journey to
   Liverpool or the journey to York?

10. Kamal's sports lesson starts at 12:30.
    He plays rounders for 20 minutes.
    Then he plays cricket for 17 minutes.
    What time does the lesson end?
    Give your answer using the 24-hour clock.

11. What time is halfway between
    9:10 am and 1:10 pm?
    Give your answer using the 12-hour clock.

Set C

Five children take it in turns to read stories to the class.
The table below shows when each child was reading.

Name	Started reading	Finished reading
Suresh	09:05	09:29
Heather	09:31	10:42
Nina	11:06	11:38
David	11:43	12:19
Emma	12:24	12:56

1. How long did Suresh read for?

2. How long did David read for?

3. Who read for longer — David or Nina?

4. Who read for the same amount of time as Nina?

5. Noah starts washing cars at 10:15 am.
   He washes cars for 3 hours 25 minutes.
   What time does he finish?
   Give your answer using the 12-hour clock.

6. A train arrives at a station at 11:05.
   It is 1 hour 27 minutes late.
   What time should it have arrived?
   Give your answer using the 24-hour clock.

7. Eve ran a marathon in 6 hours 25 minutes.
   She finished at 14:35. When did she start?
   Give your answer using the 12-hour clock.

8. Malik gets on a bus at 11:22 am.
   The clock on the right shows
   the time he got off the bus.
   How long was his bus journey?

9. Andy draws two pictures. He starts
   drawing at 6:10 pm and finishes at 7:20 pm.
   The first picture takes him 25 minutes.
   How long does the second picture take?

10. Tilly has a music lesson from 09:10 am to
    10:20 am. She plays the piano for the first
    half of the lesson and the violin for the rest.
    What time does she start playing the violin?
    Give your answer using the 12-hour clock.

11. Si bakes a cake at 2:30 pm. He bakes it for
    1 hour 2 minutes and lets it cool for 47
    minutes. What time is the cake finished?
    Give your answer using the 12-hour clock.

I can work out start and finish times and how long events take.

Measurement — Review 3

Look at the clocks below.

A   B   C

In words, write the time:

1. on clock A
2. on clock B
3. on clock C

4. five minutes after the time on clock A
5. ten minutes before the time on clock B

On a copy of the clock on the right, draw hands to show:

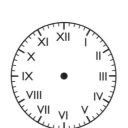

6. Quarter past eight
7. Twenty to four
8. Six minutes past ten
9. Nine minutes to one

Write the times shown on these clocks in words.
Say if the time is before noon or after noon.

10. `08:00`
11. `22:00`
12. `14:15`
13. `02:45`
14. `23:27`
15. `09:58`

Write these times using the 12-hour clock:

16. quarter to four in the morning
17. twenty past nine in the evening
18. four minutes to one in the afternoon

Write these times using the 24-hour clock:

19. half past five in the afternoon
20. twenty-five to ten in the evening
21. thirteen minutes to three in the morning

How many days are there in:

22. June?
23. September and October in total?
24. November, December and January in total?

What date is:

25. 1 day after 30th April?
26. 4 days before 2nd June?
27. a week after 30th August?

28. Chloe goes on holiday on 29th July and comes home 10 days later. What is the date when she comes home?

The table below shows the times of children in the sack race on sports day.

29. Who won the race?
30. Who came fourth?
31. How much faster was Jade than Jack?
32. How much slower was Leo than Amy?

Name	Time
Mako	1 min 52 secs
Jade	2 mins 13 secs
Amy	1 min 57 secs
Leo	2 mins 5 secs
Jack	2 mins 34 secs

33. Julie danced for 1 hour 8 minutes on Monday and 56 minutes on Tuesday. How much longer did she dance on Monday than on Tuesday?

34. Kim started her paper round at 7 am and finished 1 hour 35 minutes later. What time did she finish? Give your answer using the 12-hour clock.

The plan below shows the times that an artist paints on each day of the week.

35. How long did he paint for on Friday?

36. How long did he paint for on Monday and Tuesday in total?

Monday	09:00 - 14:30
Tuesday	09:00 - 17:00
Wednesday	09:00 - 17:00
Thursday	09:00 - 14:00
Friday	09:00 - 12:30
Saturday	09:00 - 18:30
Sunday	09:00 - 14:30

37. On which day was he painting for the longest time?

38. Nyjah left for school at 07:50. He walked for 12 minutes then got on the school bus for 20 minutes. What time did he get to school? Give your answer using the 12-hour clock.

39. Amir started boxing at 6:35 pm and finished at 8:15 pm. During that time he took a 20 minute break. How long did he spend boxing?

There were a lot of questions to do on this page — top work!

Measurement — Challenges

1. The ten weights below each have their mass written on them.

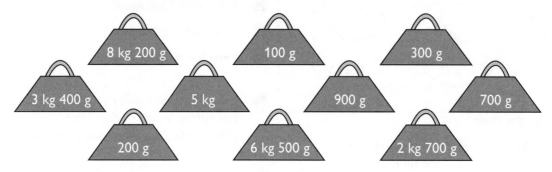

a) What is the total mass of the two heaviest weights?

b) What is the difference in mass between the heaviest and the lightest weights?

c) Which two weights have a difference in mass of 2 kg?

d) Can you find three weights that have a total mass of:

   i) 8 kg?

   ii) 4 kg 200 g?

2. It's time to make your own matching game for the months of the year. Follow these instructions:

   1. Cut up a piece of paper into 24 smaller pieces.

   2. On 12 of the pieces write all of the months of the year.

   3. On the other 12 write the number of days in each month.

   4. Turn all the pieces of paper face down.

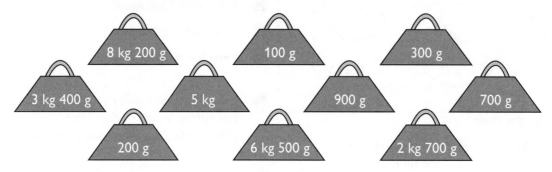

Now it's time to play — the aim is to match each month with the number of days it has.
There is one rule — you can only turn over two pieces of paper at the same time.
If they don't match then turn them back over and choose a different pair.
If they do match then you've found a pair and can move them to one side.

Challenge your friend to see how quickly they can match up all of the cards.

3. There are eight different British coins. The coins and their values are shown below.

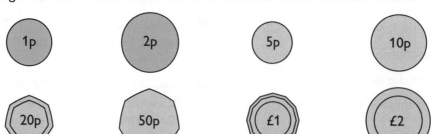

a) What is the smallest amount of money that you need:

   i) 3 or more coins to make?

   ii) 4 or more coins to make?

   iii) 5 or more coins to make?

b) Can you make every amount of money up to £1 using 5 coins or less? Explain your answer.

4 Both of these rectangles have a perimeter of 18 cm.

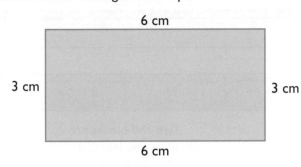

6 cm
3 cm   3 cm
6 cm

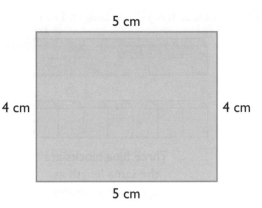

5 cm
4 cm   4 cm
5 cm

a) How many other rectangles can you draw with a perimeter of 18 cm?
The sides of your rectangles should be whole numbers of centimetres.

b) Copy and complete this table to show how many different squares
and rectangles you can make that have these perimeters.

Perimeter	4 cm	6 cm	8 cm	10 cm	12 cm	14 cm	16 cm	18 cm	20 cm
Number of different rectangles and squares									

c) Can you see a pattern in your table? Explain your answer.

5 Here are some clocks in a repair shop.

All of these clock faces are missing their minute hand. Can you estimate what time each one is showing?

a)

b)
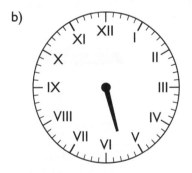

c)
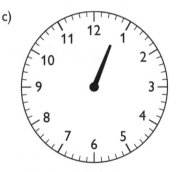

All of these digital clocks are also broken.
The descriptions tell you what is wrong with them.
Find all of the possible times that each digital clock could be showing.

d)

One of the numbers
showing hours has
stopped working.

e)

One of the numbers
showing minutes has
stopped working.

f)

Some parts are
missing from
the minutes.

Hint: this is how each number
should look on a digital clock.

Look at the yellow, blue and red blocks below.

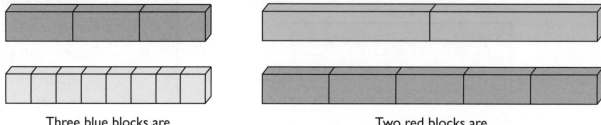

Three blue blocks are
the same length as
eight yellow blocks.

Two red blocks are
the same length as
five blue blocks.

a) If a blue block is 8 cm long:

   i) How long is a yellow block?

   ii) How long is a red block?

b) If a yellow block is 12 cm long how long are these lines of blocks? Write your answers in m and cm.

   i)

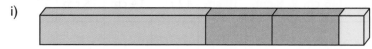

   ii)

7   Farmer Wyatt has three 4-litre buckets (green, purple and yellow), but they are all leaking.

250 ml leaks
out of the green
bucket every hour.

100 ml leaks out of
the purple bucket
every 30 minutes.

100 ml leaks out of
the yellow bucket
every 15 minutes.

At 06:00 there were 4 litres of water in each bucket.

a) How much water will be in each bucket at 07:00?

b) How much water will be in each bucket at noon?

What time will it be when:

c) the green bucket runs out of water?

d) the purple bucket is half full?

e) the yellow bucket runs out of water?

Measurement challenges complete — keep up the good work!

Turns

A quarter turn is a right angle — bigger turns like half and full turns are made up of a multiple of right angles.

Example

Harvey is in the middle of the grid on the right.

He starts facing the blue triangle and turns three right angles clockwise.

What colour of triangle is he facing now?

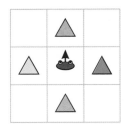

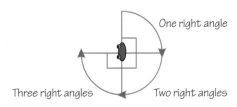

One right angle

Three right angles

Two right angles

He is facing the **yellow triangle**.

Set A

Start with ⟶ for each question.

Draw the new arrow after it has turned:

1 two right angles clockwise.

2 four right angles clockwise.

3 one right angle clockwise.

4 three right angles clockwise.

5 one right angle anticlockwise.

The arrow is pointing at the letter A in the grid on the right.

How many right angles clockwise does the arrow turn to point to the:

6 letter B?

7 letter D?

How many right angles are there in:

8 a full turn?

9 a three-quarter turn?

10 a half turn?

11 a quarter turn?

12 two full turns?

13 two quarter turns?

Set B

Use the diagram to answer the questions below.

North
West — East
South

How many quarter turns clockwise are there from:

1 North to South?

2 East to North?

3 West back to West again?

Look at the diagrams below.

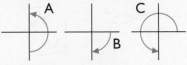

A   C
B

How many right angles are shown by arrow:

4 A?

5 B?

6 C?

Dana stands still. She says:

"There is a blue box on my right and a red box behind me."

Describe the turn she would make:

7 clockwise to look at the blue box.

8 anticlockwise to look at the red box.

Set C

Look at the windmill.

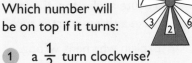

Which number will be on top if it turns:

1 a $\frac{1}{2}$ turn clockwise?

2 a $\frac{3}{4}$ turn anticlockwise?

3 two full turns clockwise?

4 a $\frac{1}{4}$ turn anticlockwise?

Amy follows these three steps:

> 1. Turn three right angles clockwise.
> 2. Turn one right angle anticlockwise.
> 3. Turn clockwise until you face the same way you started.

How many right angles:

5 did she turn in step 3?

6 did she turn in total?

Serena spins a spinning top.

How many right angles has it turned if it completes:

7 one full turn?

8 a three-quarter turn?

9 two and a half turns?

10 ten full turns?

11 one and a quarter turns?

I can recognise turns as multiples of right angles.

Acute and Obtuse Angles

'Acute' and 'obtuse' are just mathsy ways of saying that an angle is less than or greater than a right angle.

Examples

What type of angles are A, B and C?

 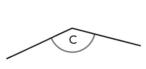 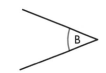 

Acute nose

Obtuse fin

A is a **right angle**.

B is an **acute angle**.
It is less than a right angle.

C is an **obtuse angle**.
It is greater than a right angle.

Set A

Look at the angles below.

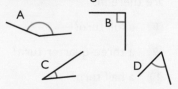

1. Which one is greater than a right angle?

2. Which two are smaller than a right angle?

Look at the angles below.

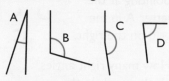

Which letters complete the sentences below?

3. ☐ and ☐ are obtuse.

4. ☐ and ☐ are acute.

5. Match the angle descriptions below to the correct shape.

3 acute angles

1 obtuse angle

4 right angles

Set B

Look at the angles below.

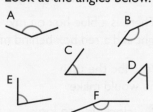

1. Which are greater than a right angle?

2. Which are smaller?

Look at the angles below.

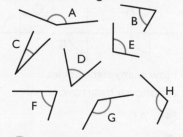

3. Which are acute?

4. Which are obtuse?

Look at the shape below.

Angle A is a right angle.

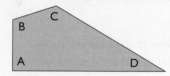

Which angles in the shape are:

5. obtuse?

6. acute?

Set C

Look at the angles below.

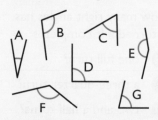

1. Which are acute?

2. Which are obtuse?

Look at the shape below.

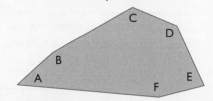

How many:

3. acute angles are there?

4. obtuse angles are there?

5. Yanis says: "You can put 3 acute angles together to make a three-quarter turn."

Explain why he is wrong.

6. Talat draws a square. He joins the opposite corners with straight lines.

How many acute angles are in his shape?

I can identify acute and obtuse angles.

Lines

Straight lines can come in all sorts of different types — these two pages will help you to tell them apart.

Examples

Look at the rectangle below.

a) Write 'vertical' or 'horizontal' to make the sentences below correct.

The purple lines are ⟨ **horizontal** ⟩.

The blue lines are ⟨ **vertical** ⟩.

b) Mark on all pairs of parallel lines.

The shape has **2 pairs** of parallel lines.

Parallel lines are shown with matching arrows.

Which pair of lines below are perpendicular?

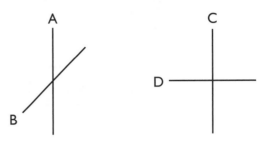

Lines **C and D** are perpendicular because they are at right angles to each other:

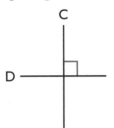

Set A

1 Look at the shapes below.

Copy and complete the table to show the number of horizontal lines and vertical lines in each shape.

Shape	Horizontal Lines	Vertical Lines
A	2	
B		1
C		

On centimetre squared paper, draw the following:

2 A pair of parallel lines.
Each line should be 5 cm long.

3 A pair of perpendicular lines.
Each line should be 4 cm long.

Look at the shapes below.
Each side is labelled with a letter.

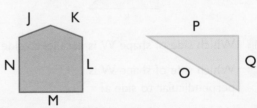

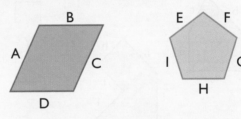

Write down the letters of all:

4 horizontal sides.

5 vertical sides.

Rewrite the sentences with 'parallel' or 'perpendicular' in each gap:

6 Sides A and C are ⟨ ⟩.

7 Sides M and N are ⟨ ⟩.

8 Sides P and Q are ⟨ ⟩.

Look at the shapes below.

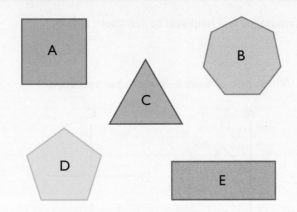

Copy out the shapes below on centimetre squared paper.

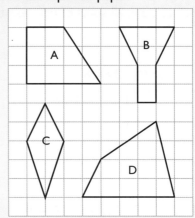

Are the following statements true or false?

① "All the shapes have at least one horizontal line."

② "All the shapes have at least one pair of parallel lines."

③ "None of the shapes have any perpendicular lines."

④ "There are 7 vertical lines in total."

⑤ "There are 7 horizontal lines in total."

⑥ Mark every pair of parallel lines with arrows.

⑦ Add right angles to show any perpendicular lines in these shapes.

Look at the lines on the right.

Measure the length:

⑧ of the vertical line.

⑨ of the horizontal line.

Look at the shapes below.

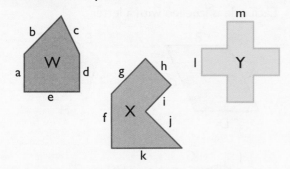

Copy out the incomplete shapes below on centimetre squared paper.

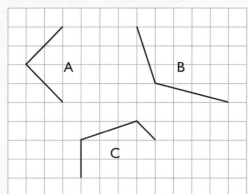

Draw 2 lines to make a complete shape:

⑨ Shape A should have two pairs of parallel lines.

⑩ Shape B should have two pairs of parallel lines.

⑪ Shape C should have one line that is perpendicular to two other lines.

① Which side of shape W is parallel to side d?

② Which side of shape W is perpendicular to side a?

③ Which sides of shape W are vertical?

④ Which side of shape X is parallel to side j?

⑤ Which side of shape X is horizontal?

⑥ Which two sides of shape X are perpendicular to side h?

⑦ How many sides of shape Y are parallel to side m?

⑧ How many sides of shape Y are vertical?

⑫ On centimetre squared paper, draw a vertical line that is 4 cm long and a line perpendicular to it that is 6 cm long.

I can identify horizontal, vertical, parallel and perpendicular lines.

Geometry — Review 1

① Lee is on a roundabout.
His starting position is shown
in the picture on the right.

Match Lee's finishing position
to the correct anticlockwise turn.

three-quarter turn   half turn

     quarter turn   full turn

   A   B   C   D

Complete these sentences:

② Turning 3 right angles is the same as a ☐ turn.

③ Turning 1 right angle is the same as a ☐ turn.

④ Turning 2 right angles is the same as a ☐ turn.

⑤ Turning 4 right angles is the same as a ☐ turn.

Look at the compass on the right.

Which direction would you
be facing if you turn:

North
West ←→ East
South

⑥ two right angles clockwise from East?

⑦ four right angles clockwise from South?

⑧ one right angle anticlockwise from South?

⑨ three right angles anticlockwise from West?

The grid below shows four moons.

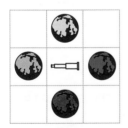

Tom looks through his telescope
and can see the red moon.

How many right angles clockwise
does he need to turn to see:

⑩ the blue moon?

⑪ the yellow moon?

Look at the angles below:

  A   B   C   D   E   F   G

⑫ Which of the angles is a right angle?

⑬ Which of the angles are obtuse?

⑭ Which of the angles are acute?

Look at the shapes below.

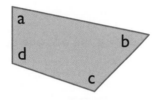 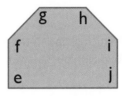

Which angles in the shapes are:

⑮ acute?

⑯ obtuse?

Copy out the shapes below on centimetre squared paper.

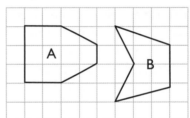

How many:

⑰ horizontal lines are there in total?

⑱ vertical lines are there in total?

⑲ Mark the pairs of parallel lines
in shape A with arrows.

Look at the shapes below.

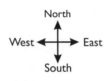 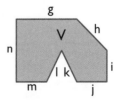

⑳ Which side of shape U is parallel to side c?

㉑ Which side of shape U is horizontal?

㉒ Which sides of shape V are perpendicular to side n?

㉓ Which sides of shape V are vertical?

Those questions had a lot of twisting and turning! Well done — hope you're not too dizzy.

Describing 2D Shapes

"2D" means "2 dimensional", which is just a fancy maths way of saying that a shape is flat.
You can use your knowledge of lines and angles to help you identify and describe different 2D shapes.

Examples

What is the name of the shape below?
How many angles does it have?

Count the number of sides and angles.

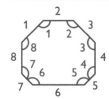

It is an **octagon** — there are **8 sides** and **8 angles**.

Which shape in the row below is the odd one out?
Explain your answer.

Shape C is the odd one out.

Shape C has 4 sides.
Shapes A, B and D have 5 sides (they are pentagons).

Set A

Match the names below to the letter of the correct 2D shape on the right.

1. quadrilateral

2. circle

3. triangle

4. octagon

5. pentagon

6. hexagon

7. semi-circle

8. Look at the shapes below.

Copy and complete the table by putting a tick or a cross in every box for each shape.

	four or more sides	at least one right angle	three or more equal angles
A			
B			
C			
D			

Measure the sides of the pentagon below.

Complete the sentences:

9. "The shape has ☐ pairs of equal sides."

10. "The longest pair of equal sides are ☐ cm long."

Set B

1   Look at the shapes below.

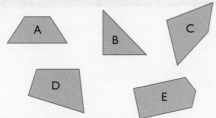

Copy and complete the table by putting the letters of each shape in the correct place. One has been done for you.

	quadrilateral	not a quadrilateral
one pair of parallel lines	A	
no parallel lines		

What is the name of each shape described below?

2   "I have three straight sides."

3   "I have four right angles and two pairs of equal parallel sides."

4   "I have five sides that are different lengths."

Look at the shapes below.

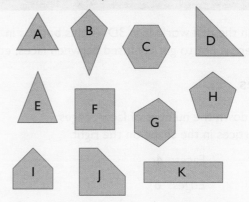

5   Which shapes have all equal sides?

6   Which shapes have right angles?

7   Which shapes have no pairs of parallel lines?

8   Which shapes are pentagons?

9   Which shapes are hexagons?

10 Measure the sides of the shape below.

Describe the number and length of the pairs of equal length sides in the shape.

Set C

Write down the number of sides and angles in the shapes below:

1   quadrilateral

2   pentagon

Look at these shapes.

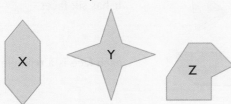

Describe each shape by completing the sentences:

3   X has ☐ angles and ☐ sides.
    It is called ☐.

4   Y has ☐ angles and ☐ sides.
    It is called ☐.

5   Z has ☐ angles and ☐ sides.
    It is called ☐.

For each row of shapes, find the odd one out. Explain your answer.

Hint: think about the number of sides in the shapes, the types of angles and the types of lines.

6 | A | B | C | D

7 | E | F | G | H

8   Measure the sides of this shape:

Describe the number and the length of the sides in the shape.

I can recognise and describe 2D shapes.

Describing 3D Shapes

Everything in the real world is in 3D — this book is in 3D, and so are you!
The trick here is not to get confused between faces, edges and vertices.

Examples

Write down the number of faces, edges
and vertices in the shape on the right.

Faces: **4**

Edges: **6**

Vertices: **4**

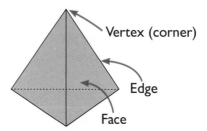

Vertex (corner)

Edge

Face

Look at the 3D shapes below.

A   B

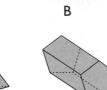

C   D

Which shape has 5 vertices?   Shape **A**

Which shapes have triangular faces?   Shapes **A** and **C**

What is the total number of edges on shapes B and C?

Shape B has 12 edges and shape C has 9 edges.
So in total they have 12 + 9 = **21 edges**.

Set A

Look at the shapes below.

A   B   C   D

E   F   G   H

Which is the correct name
from the box for shape:

1 E?

2 G?

3 H?

| cube | sphere |
| cuboid | tetrahedron |

4 Which shapes are prisms?

5 Which shape has two circular faces?

6 Which shape has two square faces?

7 Which shape has eight vertices?

8 Match each of the 3D shapes
below to the correct property:

        it has one circular face

        it has six faces

        each face is a triangle

        it has no flat surfaces

Complete the sentence to
describe the shape on the right:

9 The shape has ☐ faces,
☐ vertices and
☐ edges. Two of
its faces are ☐.

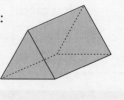

Look at the 3D shapes and shape names below.

A   B   C

Which is the correct name for shape:

1. A?

2. B?

3. C?

4. How many faces does shape C have?

5. How many edges does shape A have?

6. What is the total number of vertices in shapes A and C?

7. Aled is thinking of a 3D shape.
   It has one circular face.

   Write down two different shapes he could be thinking of.

Look at the 3D shapes below.

A   B   C   D

E   F   G   H

8. Which shape has two circular faces?

9. Which shapes have at least one triangular face?

10. Which shape has 8 edges?

11. Which shapes have 5 faces?

12. Tilly has a prism.
    The two end faces of her prism are pentagons.

    Complete the sentence:

    "Tilly's prism has ☐ faces and ☐ vertices."

Set C

Name the 3D shape from its picture or description below.

1.

2.

3. "I have all square faces and 8 vertices."

4. "I have 1 square face and 8 edges."

5. "I have 2 circular faces."

How many faces do the following shapes have?

6. a cylinder

7. a cuboid

8. a hemisphere

9. a pentagonal prism

10. a heptagonal prism

Work out the total number of faces, edges and vertices in each of the following shapes:

11. a square-based pyramid

12. a triangular prism

13. a tetrahedron

14. an octagonal prism

Some 3D shapes are described below, but some of the words are missing. Complete the sentences.

15. This prism has 12 vertices.
    Its two end faces are ☐.
    It has ☐ faces in total and ☐ edges.
    It is called ☐.

16. This shape has 8 triangular faces.
    It has ☐ vertices and ☐ edges.
    It is called ☐.

I can recognise and describe 3D shapes.

Drawing 2D Shapes

You should be pretty good at recognising and describing 2D shapes by now.
You need to be able to draw loads of different 2D shapes too — the examples below will get you started...

Examples

Complete the octagon on the grid below.

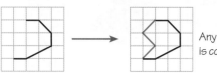

Any 8-sided shape
is correct here.

Use centimetre squared paper to draw
a rectangle with a side 3 cm long.

One square on the grid is 1 cm,
so one side of the rectangle
should be 3 squares long.

Set A

Copy and complete the shapes below.
Use centimetre squared paper.

1 square

2 rectangle

3 pentagon

4 hexagon

On centimetre squared paper,
draw the following shapes:

5 a square with sides of 2 cm

6 a triangle with
two sides of 3 cm

7 a rectangle with one side of
4 cm and one side of 2 cm

8 a rectangle with one side of
6 cm and one side of 5 cm

Set B

Copy and complete the shapes below.
Use centimetre squared paper.

1 triangle

2 pentagon

3 heptagon

4 octagon

On centimetre squared paper,
draw the following shapes:

5 a triangle with a right angle

6 a triangle with two
sides of equal length

7 a triangle with no sides
of equal length

8 a square with sides
of 3 cm 5 mm

Set C

Copy the dots onto centimetre
squared paper for each question.

Join the dots with straight lines
to make the following shapes:

1 an octagon

2 a pentagon with two pairs
of equal length sides

3 a hexagon with a side of 6 cm

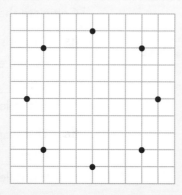

On centimetre squared paper,
draw the following shapes:

4 a quadrilateral with
two sides of 5 cm and
two sides of 3 cm

5 a hexagon with one
pair of parallel sides

6 a heptagon with one
side of 3 cm 5 mm

I can draw 2D shapes.

Making 3D Shapes

Time to move back to 3D — these pages will make you think about how to make 3D shapes of your own.

Examples

How many sticks and balls of clay do you need to create the 3D shape below?

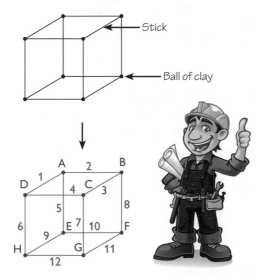

You need **12 sticks** (1-12) and **8 balls of clay** (A-H).

How many cubes would you need to build the shape below?

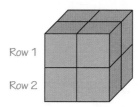

There are 2 rows of 2 cubes at the front:
$2 \times 2 = 4$ cubes

The cuboid is 2 cubes deep, so there are
$4 \times 2 = 8$ cubes in total

You would need **8 cubes** to build this shape.

Set A

The shapes below are made out of sticks and balls of clay.

Complete the sentences:

You have lots of these cubes:

How many cubes would you need to make each of the cuboids below?

1. Shape A is made of
   ☐ sticks and
   ☐ balls of clay.

A

2. Shape B is made of
   ☐ sticks and
   ☐ balls of clay.

B

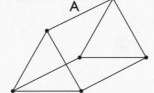

3. Shape C is made of
   ☐ sticks and
   ☐ balls of clay.

C

4. Shape D is made of
   ☐ sticks and
   ☐ balls of clay.

D

5.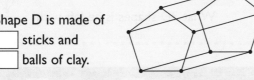

6.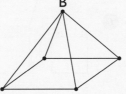

7.

8.

9.

The shapes below are made out of sticks and balls of clay.

Complete the sentences:

1 Shape A is made of
☐ sticks and
☐ balls of clay.

 A

2 Shape B is made of
☐ sticks and
☐ balls of clay.

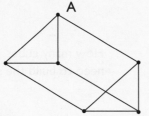 B

3 Shape C is made of
☐ sticks and
☐ balls of clay.

 C

How many more cubes would you need to make the second cuboid than the first cuboid?

4

5

Look at the groups of card shapes below. For each group, write down what 3D shape you could make using the cards.

6

7

You have lots of these cubes:

 1 cm, 1 cm, 1 cm

Work out how many cubes you would need to build each of the shapes below.

1 ☐ cubes

2 ☐ cubes

3 ☐ cubes 2 cm 1 cm 3 cm

4 ☐ cubes 2 cm 2 cm 2 cm

Look at the groups of card shapes below. For each group, write down what 3D shape you could make using the cards.

5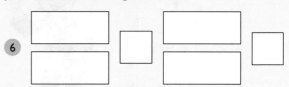

6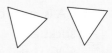

7 Khaled makes the shape on the right out of sticks and balls of clay.

He removes the four red sticks and is left with two identical shapes.

What 3D shapes is he left with?

I can make 3D shapes with modelling materials.

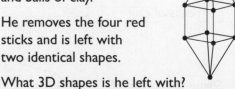

Geometry — Review 2

Carla thinks of two 2D shapes.

"This shape has four right angles and four equal sides."

(1) What shape is she thinking of?

"This shape has six sides and no sides are equal."

(2) What is the second shape she is thinking of?

For each row of shapes, find the odd one out.
Explain your answer.

(3)

(4)

Look at the prisms below.

A   B   C

Complete the sentences:

(5) Shape A has ☐ edges,
☐ faces and ☐ vertices.

(6) Shape B has ☐ edges,
☐ faces and ☐ vertices.

(7) Shape C has ☐ edges,
☐ faces and ☐ vertices.

Angela describes three different 3D shapes. Use her
descriptions below to work out what the shapes are.

(8) "It has six square faces."

(9) "It has three triangular faces."

(10) "It has one circular face and no vertices."

Copy and complete the shapes below.
Use centimetre squared paper.

(11) 1 rectangle

(12) 1 pentagon

(13) 1 heptagon

(14) 1 triangle and 1 square

Look at the shapes below.

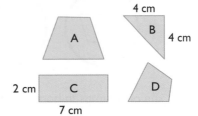

(15) Which shape is not a quadrilateral?

(16) Which shapes have at least one right angle?

On centimetre squared paper, draw:

(17) shape B   (18) shape C

On centimetre squared paper, draw:

(19) a rectangle with a shortest side of 1 cm.

(20) a square with sides of 4 cm 5 mm.

(21) How many cubes would you need
to make each of the shapes below?

A   B   C

How many sticks and balls of clay would
you need to make the following shapes:

(22) a tetrahedron?

(23) a cuboid?

(24) a square-based pyramid?

(25) a hexagonal prism?

Describing, recognising, drawing, modelling... you've covered it all — fantastic work!

Geometry — Challenges

1 Erica is taking part in a playground game.

She starts on the left and has to jump in a red hoop, a blue hoop, a purple hoop, and end in a green hoop.

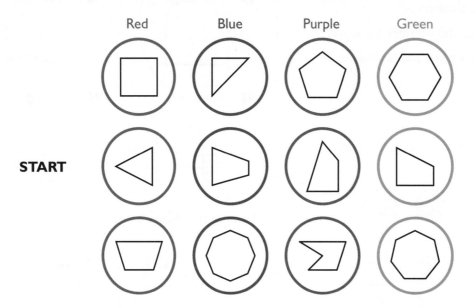

Red   Blue   Purple   Green

START

On her first go, she only jumps in hoops that show a shape with at least one right angle.

a) Which path did she take?

On her second go, she only jumps in hoops that show a shape with one pair of parallel lines.

b) Which path did she take this time?

2 Get into groups of 4 for this activity.
Each person will need a different coloured pen, pencil or crayon.

You will need an 8 × 8 dotted grid like the one below.

Decide who is player 1, 2, 3 and 4 and follow the steps below to draw a line between two dots in your colour:

- A player must draw from the <u>end of another line</u> and is <u>not</u> allowed to <u>cross over</u> another line.

- Player 1 draws a vertical or horizontal line.

- Player 2 draws a diagonal line (half a right angle).

- Player 3 draws a line parallel to Player 2's line.

- Player 4 draws a line perpendicular to Player 3's line.

- Start from Player 1 again.

How long can you keep going until a player can't draw a line?
Play again and see if you can keep drawing for longer!

3 Get into groups of 3 or 4 to play this game.

Write the names of all the shapes below on separate small pieces of card.

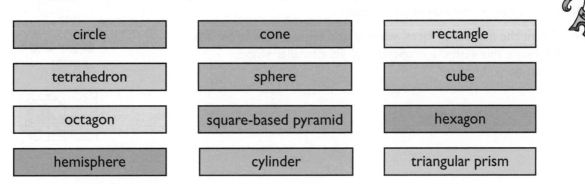

circle	cone	rectangle
tetrahedron	sphere	cube
octagon	square-based pyramid	hexagon
hemisphere	cylinder	triangular prism

Here's how you play the game:

* Put all the cards face down and mix them up.

* One person takes a card (without showing anyone else) and describes the shape, without saying its name.

* The first person to guess what shape is being described wins the card.

* A new person picks up a card and everyone else gets ready to guess again.

* The winner is the person with the most cards when there are none left to pick.

4 Wilfred the worm is lost.
There are four tunnels he can choose from, but only one leads home.

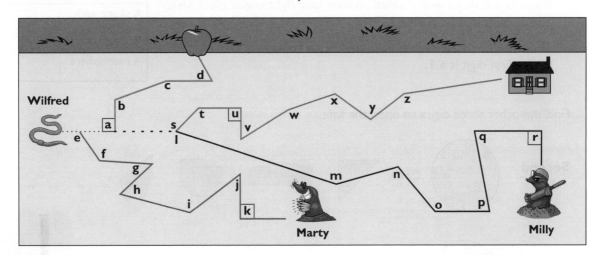

Wilfred goes through one tunnel and finds the apple.

a) How many of each type of angle did he turn through?

Wilfred goes back to where he started and tries a second tunnel.
He counts the number of acute angles he turns through.

b) Milly's tunnel has 2 acute angles, so Wilfred knows he is in Marty's tunnel before he reaches the end.
    Where in Marty's tunnel does he know this?

Wilfred tries a third tunnel and finds his way home.

c) How many obtuse angles does he turn through in the third tunnel?

5 Build a 3D shape out of cubes.

a) Record the number of faces, vertices and edges it has.

Now, build a larger version of your shape.

b) Count the number of faces, vertices and edges of the larger shape.
Compare this with the properties of your smaller shape.
What do you notice?

Example

Small Shape

Larger Shape

6 Mr Nugget, the bank manager, has forgotten how to get into his safe!
Luckily, a code of shapes tells him the correct four digits he needs.

The key on the right tells you how to turn the dial and find the digits.

He has worked out the first digit for you:

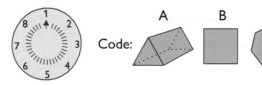

Code:

A   B   C

Shape A is a prism, so turn two right angles anticlockwise.
The arrow turns from **1** to **5**.

Shape B is a shape with 4 sides, so turn two right angles clockwise.
The arrow turns from **5** to **1**.

Shape C is a shape with 7 sides, so turn four right angles clockwise.
The arrow turns from **1** to **1**.

There are no more shapes, so there are no turns left.
So the first digit is a **1**.

Key	
Turn clockwise for a 2D shape.	
Turn anticlockwise for a 3D shape.	
A shape with 3 sides	Turn one right angle
A sphere	
A shape with 4 sides	Turn two right angles
A prism	
A shape with 5 or 6 sides	Turn three right angles
A pyramid	
A shape with 7 or 8 sides	Turn four right angles
A hemisphere	

Find the other three digits to open the safe.

Second digit   Code:

Third digit   Code:

Fourth digit   Code:

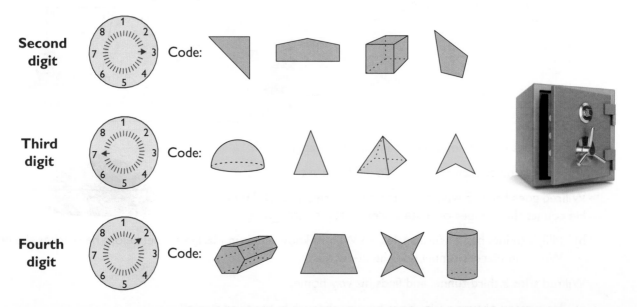

Well done — your geometry skills will be in top shape after those tricky challenges!

Tables

Tables are not just a handy surface to rest your dinner on. In maths, tables are used to collect information (data) in a way that makes it easier to understand. Tally charts are a useful type of table.

Examples

Tom saw the following things at the beach one day:

Fill in the table below to show the number of each thing he found.

What Tom saw	Tally	Frequency
Crabs	||	2
Fossils	|||	3
Jellyfish	||||	4
Shells	⽕⼑ |	6

Frequency is the number of tallies for each category. It tells you how many of each thing there are.

Use the table to work out how many animals Tom saw.

The animals are crabs and jellyfish:

Number of crabs = 2   Number of jellyfish = 4

Total number of animals = 2 + 4 = **6 animals**

Set A

Pip empties out her pencil case and finds the following things:

She makes a tally chart and starts to fill it in:

	Tally
Pencils	||||
Pens	
Rulers	
Marbles	

1. Make a copy of the tally chart. Fill in the tallies for the other rows.

2. Add up the number of tallies for each row.

3. Use the table to write down the number of pencils in Pip's pencil case.

4. What thing does Pip have most of in her pencil case? (Use the table to help.)

A painter makes a tally chart to record the number of pots of paint he has of each colour:

Colour	Tally	Number of pots
White	⽕⼑ ||	7
Blue	|||	
Yellow	⽕⼑	
Green	|||	

5. Copy and complete the table.

Copy and complete these sentences:

6. There is the same amount of green paint as ☐ paint.

7. There are ☐ pots of white and blue paint altogether.

8. Copy and complete the following table:

Jo's pets	Tally	Frequency
Dogs	||	☐
Cats	☐	4
Rabbits	⽕⼑ |	☐

Set B

Mark is in the park.
He sees the following animals:

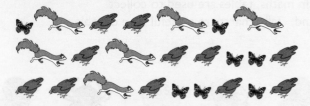

He records the first three animals he sees in the tally chart below:

Animal	Tally	Frequency
Butterfly	I	
Squirrel	I	
Bird	I	

1) Copy Mark's table and complete the tallies.

2) Add up the tallies to fill in the frequency column.

3) What was the animal that Mark saw the most in the park?

4) How many animals did Mark see in total?

Lola recorded what she ate for breakfast every day for 30 days in the table below:

Breakfast	Tally	Frequency
Cereal	IIII IIII I	
Toast		10
Eggs	II	
Crumpets		7

5) Copy and complete Lola's table.

True or false?

6) Lola ate toast more often than crumpets.

7) Lola ate eggs the least.

8) Lola ate cereal less often than toast.

Over the next six days, Lola ate for breakfast:

Eggs Toast Crumpets Toast Crumpets Eggs

9) What did Lola eat most often over 36 days?

Set C

Heidi asks children in her class what their favourite colour is. Here are their answers:

Blue Red Blue Pink Red Blue Gold Red
Red Red Pink Gold Blue Pink Red Blue
Pink Pink Blue Blue Red Blue Red Red
Blue Gold Pink Red Red Red Blue Pink

She makes the table below to record the information:

Colour	Tally	Frequency
Blue		
Red		
Pink		
☐		

1) What colour is missing?

2) Copy Heidi's table and fill in all the missing information.

3) What is the least popular colour?

4) How many people does Heidi ask?

Twenty people were asked:
"How many sisters and brothers do you have?"
The results are shown in the table below:

Number of sisters and brothers	Frequency
0	6
1	8
2	4
3 or more	2

True or false?

5) Six people had no sisters and brothers.

6) Eight people had two sisters and brothers.

7) "One" was the most common answer.

8) The most common answer had double the frequency of the least common answer.

Fred wants to know how many people have one sister and one brother.

9) Explain why he can't get this information from the table.

I can interpret and present data in tables.

Bar Charts

Bar charts are a great way to display the data from tables. The height of the bar tells you the number of something.

Examples

A group of friends love reading books.

The table below shows the number of books each friend reads over six months.

Show this information on a bar chart.

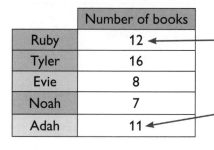

	Number of books
Ruby	12
Tyler	16
Evie	8
Noah	7
Adah	11

Ruby reads 12 books, so the bar goes up to 12 on the scale.

Adah reads 11 books, so the bar is halfway between 10 and 12.

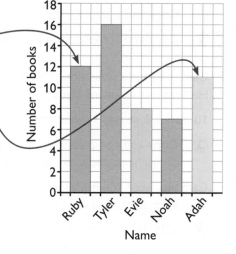

Shaan adds another bar to the chart to show the number of books he read.

How many books did Shaan read?

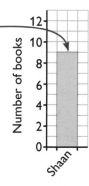

The bar is halfway between 8 and 10 on the scale.

So Shaan read **9 books**.

Set A

A bird rescue centre has four types of owl. The bar chart on the right shows the number of two of the types of owl.

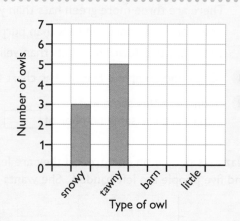

1. How many snowy owls are there?

2. How many tawny owls are there?

There are 6 barn owls and 1 little owl. Copy and complete the bar chart to show:

3. the number of barn owls.

4. the number of little owls.

Suki sorts her socks. She records how many pairs of each design she has in the table below:

Sock design	Number of pairs of socks
red spots	5
blue stripes	3
purple stars	8
plain pink	6

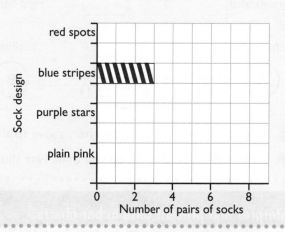

5. Copy and complete the bar chart on the right with the information in the table.

Sara sells sandwiches with different fillings.
She records how many of each type she sells in
the table below, and on the bar chart on the right.

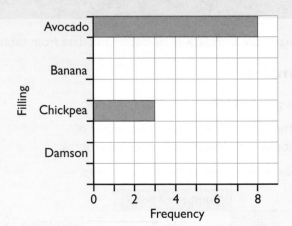

Sandwich filling	Frequency
Avocado	☐
Banana	5
Chickpea	☐
Damson	2

1. Copy and complete the table.

2. Copy and complete the bar chart.

Cam goes for a walk along a canal.
He sees the following birds:

10 ducks, 6 geese, 5 swans and a heron.

3. Copy and complete the bar chart on
the right to show this information.

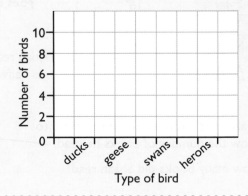

Cam also sees some magpies on his walk.
The number of magpies is half the number of geese.

4. Add this information to the bar chart.

Set C

Harry has a lot of hats. He starts to make a bar chart showing the different colours of his hats:
Here are some facts about Harry's hats:

- There are twice as many red hats as yellow hats.
- There are three more green hats than yellow hats.
- There are two more red hats than purple hats.
- There are two fewer blue hats than yellow hats.

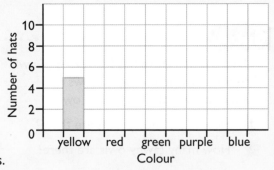

1. Copy and complete Harry's bar chart using these facts.

2. Complete this sentence:
   There are the same number of ☐ hats as ☐ hats.

Naz asks people on her street if they are left-handed or right-handed. Twelve people are right-handed
and five people are left-handed. She wants to present this in a bar chart, and tries different scales:

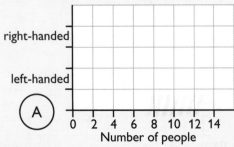 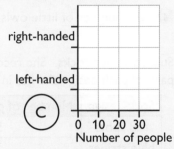 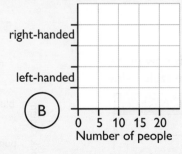

3. Copy and complete each bar chart above to show the number of right-handed and left-handed people.

4. Which chart, A, B or C, do you think Naz should use? Explain your answer.

I can interpret and present data in bar charts.

Pictograms

Like bar charts, pictograms are a way of showing amounts of things. They use symbols or pictures to stand for a certain number of things.

Examples

For each week of the summer holidays, Joy records how many of the days are sunny.

She makes a pictogram to show the information: ⟶

key: 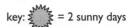 = 2 sunny days

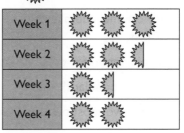

Week 1	
Week 2	
Week 3	
Week 4	

In Week 5 there were 4 sunny days, and in Week 6 there were 3 sunny days.

Add this information to the pictogram.

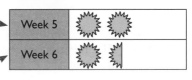

| Week 5 | |
| Week 6 | |

4 sunny days = 2 × 2 sunny days = 2 ×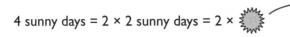

If ☀ is 2 sunny days then ▌ is 1 sunny day.

So 3 sunny days = 2 + 1 sunny days = ☀ + ▌

Which week was the sunniest? How many sunny days were there that week?

Looking at the pictogram, **Week 1** has the most suns, so it was the sunniest.

Week 1 has 3 suns. Each sun means 2 sunny days.

So there were 3 × 2 = **6 sunny days** in Week 1.

Set A

Sally grows strawberries in her garden. Each morning, she picks the ripe strawberries, and records how many she picks in a pictogram, shown on the right.

1. How many strawberries did she pick on Monday?

2. How many did she pick on Tuesday and Wednesday altogether?

On Thursday she picked 5 strawberries and on Friday she picked 2 strawberries.

3. Complete the pictogram for these days.

4. On which day did Sally pick the most strawberries?

key: 🍓 = 1 strawberry

Monday	🍓 🍓 🍓 🍓 🍓 🍓
Tuesday	🍓 🍓 🍓
Wednesday	🍓 🍓 🍓 🍓
Thursday	
Friday	

Bertie has a lot of bow ties. The pictogram on the right shows how many he has of each colour.

5. How many green bow ties does Bertie have?

6. How many purple bow ties does Bertie have?

Bertie has four blue bow ties.

7. Complete the pictogram for the blue bow ties.

8. How many bow ties does Bertie have in total?

key: 🎀 = 2 bow ties

green	🎀
orange	🎀 🎀 🎀 🎀
purple	🎀 🎀 🎀
blue	

A baker sells cupcakes in five different flavours.
He makes a pictogram, shown on the right, to record
the number of each flavour he sells in one day.

key: = 2 cupcakes

1 How many lemon cupcakes did he sell?

2 How many chocolate cupcakes did he sell?

The baker sold four caramel cupcakes and
three almond cupcakes.

3 Complete the pictogram for these flavours.

4 What was the least popular flavour?

5 How many of the two most popular flavours
did he sell altogether?

vanilla	
lemon	
chocolate	
caramel	
almond	

Pupils in a school are put into one of four teams:
Ants, Bats, Cats or Dogs. The numbers in each
team are shown in the table below.

Team:	Ants	Bats	Cats	Dogs
Number of pupils:	32	20	26	19

key: = 5 pupils

Ants	
Bats	
Cats	
Dogs	

6 Copy and complete the pictogram on the right
to show the number of pupils in each team.

The pictogram on the right shows the total number
of awards won by each year in a school.

key: = 3 awards

1 Which school year won the fewest awards?

2 Which school year won the second
largest number of awards?

3 How many awards were won by each year?

4 Show the same information on another
pictogram, using the key shown below.

key: = 4 awards

Y3	
Y4	
Y5	
Y6	

Kitty wants to show the information in the table
on the right as a pictogram, using the key below:

Key: = 10 cats

5 What is the problem with using this key?

6 What would be a better key for Kitty to use?
Show how you would use it for Matt's cats.

Name of friend	Number of cats they own
Cate	4
Tabitha	3
Tom	2
Matt	9

7 The pictogram on the right shows
that 70 people saw a show on Friday.
Complete the key: = ☐ people.

Friday	🧍 🧍 🧍 🧍 🧍 🧍 🧍

I can interpret and present data in pictograms.

Statistics — Review 1

Lin records the flowers he finds in a field:

He records them in the table below:

Flower		Tally	Frequency
Daisy	🌼		
Dandelion	🌼		
Clover	🌿		

1. Copy the table and fill in the tallies.

2. Fill in the frequency column of the table.

3. Which flower did Lin see the most?

4. Which flower did Lin see the least?

5. How many flowers did Lin see in total?

Aria, Ben and Chloe mark a tally next to their name in a table each time they eat a piece of fruit. The table is shown below, with some gaps:

	Tally	Number of pieces of fruit
Aria	IIII	☐
Ben	☐	4
Chloe	IIII I	☐

6. Copy the table and fill in the gaps.

7. Who has eaten the most fruit?

They want to display this information on a bar chart. Aria draws her own bar on the chart below:

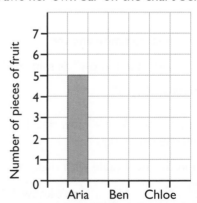

8. Copy and complete the bar chart by drawing in the bars for Ben and Chloe.

The bar chart below shows the number of each type of medal won by one team in a sports contest:

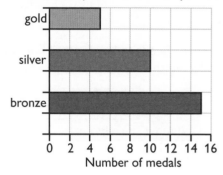

9. How many of each type of medal did they win?

10. Copy and complete the bar chart on the right with the same information.

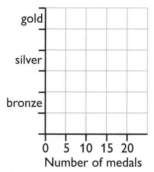

A group of children were asked to say what they most liked to play on in the playground. Their answers are shown below.

key: ❤ = 2 children

swings	❤ ❤ ❤ ❤
roundabout	❤ ❘
slide	❤ ❤ ❤ ❤ ❤ ❘
see-saw	

Four children said they liked the see-saw the most.

11. Copy and complete the pictogram.

12. What was the least common answer?

13. How many children liked the swings the most?

14. How many children liked the slide the most?

Look at the pictogram. How many oranges are squeezed in total over the weekend if the symbol ⬤ stands for:

15. 2 oranges?

16. 4 oranges?

17. 5 oranges?

18. 10 oranges?

	Oranges squeezed that day
Sat	⬤ ⬤ ⬤ ⬤
Sun	⬤ ⬤ ⬤ ⬤ ⬤ ⬤

That was a lot of data to sort out — but you did it!

Solving Problems with Tables

You might see data given in different types of tables.
The trick is to know how to read them to get the information you need.

Examples

A football coach needs to buy football boots for the children in her team.
She has collected their shoe sizes in the table below:

Shoe size:	1	2	3	4	5
Number of children:	2	1	4	2	1

How many more children need a size 3 than a size 4?

Number of children who need a size 3 = 4

Number of children who need a size 4 = 2   So 4 – 2 = **2 more** children **need a size 3**

Each child needs one pair of boots. How many boots are needed in total?

The number of pairs of boots is equal to the total number of children.

Add up all the numbers in the 'Number of children' row: 2 + 1 + 4 + 2 + 1 = 10 pairs

There are 2 boots in a pair: 10 pairs × 2 = **20 boots**

Set A

Shu counts the sweets of each colour in a bag.
She records them in the table below:

Colour	Number of sweets
Green	5
Red	3
Purple	2
Yellow	6
Orange	4

1   How many more yellow sweets are there than red?

2   How many fewer purple sweets are there than orange?

3   True or false?
    There are twice as many green sweets as red.

Shu's favourite colour is green.
She eats three sweets of this colour.

4   How many green sweets are left?

5   How many sweets are left in total?

A teacher asked his class:
"Is maths your favourite lesson?"
The answers are shown in the table below:

Answer:	Yes	No	Don't know
Frequency:	15	10	5

6   How many more said "yes" than said "no"?

True or false?

7   "Yes" was the most common answer.

8   Twice as many said "don't know" as said "no".

9   Half of the class said "yes".

Two people who said "don't know" now decide.
One says "yes" and the other says "no".

10   Copy and fill in this new table with these answers:

Answer:	Yes	No	Don't know
Frequency:			3

11   How many fewer said "no" than said "yes" in the new table?

The hair colours of children in a school are shown in the table below:

Hair:	Black	Brown	Blond	Red
Frequency:	30	35	25	10

1. How many more children have black hair than red hair?

2. How many fewer children have blond hair than brown hair?

3. How many children are in the school?

4. How many children do <u>not</u> have blond hair?

Five more children join the school.
Two have black hair, one has red hair and the others have brown hair.

5. How many new children have brown hair?

6. How many children <u>in total</u> have brown hair?

7. Copy and fill in the table below to include the new children:

Hair:	Black	Brown	Blond	Red
Frequency:				

Asif gets gold stars at school for good work.
He can get up to 3 stars a day.
The table below shows how many days in one month he got 0, 1, 2 or 3 stars:

Number of stars	Number of days
0	8
1	8
2	3
3	2

8. On how many days did Asif get at least 1 star?

9. On how many days did he get more than 1 star?

10. How many stars did he get in total?

11. A farmer has twice as many hens as ducks, and three more ducks than geese. The number of peacocks is half of the number of geese.
Copy and fill in the following table for the farmer:

Bird:	Hen	Duck	Goose	Peacock
Frequency:		5		

The Year 3 netball team played eighteen matches. Their results are shown in the table below:

Result:	Win	Lose	Draw
Frequency:	8	?	4

1. How many matches did they lose?

2. How many matches did they <u>not win</u>?

Teams get points as follows:

• Each win = 2 points

• Each draw = 1 point

• No points for losing

3. Work out how many points the Year 3 team had after eighteen matches.

The Year 4 netball team had the following results:

Result:	Win	Lose	Draw
Frequency:	10	3	5

4. How many more points did the Year 4 team have than the Year 3 team?

Lucy likes counting spots on ladybirds.
The table below shows the number of ladybirds she saw in one year with different numbers of spots:

Number of spots	Frequency
2-4	9
5-7	7
8-10	3
More than 10	1

5. How many ladybirds did Lucy see that year?

6. How many ladybirds had more than 7 spots?

7. How many ladybirds had fewer than 8 spots?

8. Lucy says, "I saw four ladybirds with ten spots." Explain why she is wrong.

9. Look at the following table:

Do you like cats?	Yes	No
Girls' answers:	6	4
Boys' answers:	5	5

Write three different statements comparing the data in this table.

I can solve problems using information in tables.

Solving Problems with Bar Charts

A bar chart can give you a lot of information. Make sure you read the scale carefully though, otherwise you won't get the information you're meant to.

Examples

Mei has a garden lamp. Each evening she finds moths on the lamp.

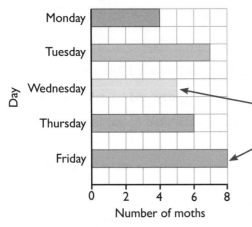

The bar chart shows the number of moths on the lamp each evening during one week.

How many more moths were on the lamp on Friday than on Wednesday?

On Wednesday there were 5 moths.

On Friday there were 8 moths.

So there were 8 − 5 = **3 more moths on Friday**.

How many moths did she see altogether on Monday and Tuesday?

On Monday there were 4 moths. On Tuesday there were 7 moths.

So in total there were 4 + 7 = **11 moths** on Monday and Tuesday.

Set A

The bar chart below shows the number of different types of biscuit in a tin:

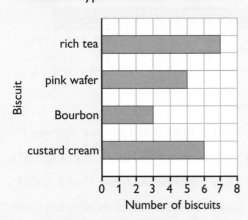

1. How many more rich tea biscuits are there than pink wafers?

2. How many fewer Bourbons are there than custard creams?

3. How many biscuits are there in total in the tin?

4. How many biscuits are <u>not</u> pink wafers?

5. Bea says, "There are half as many Bourbons as rich tea biscuits." Is she right?

A tub contains 36 crayons in five different colours, as shown on the bar chart below:

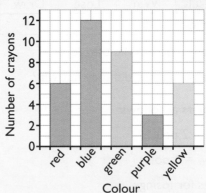

Copy the sentences and fill in the gaps with words:

6. The colour with the most crayons is ☐. There are ☐ crayons of this colour.

7. The colour with the least crayons is ☐. There are ☐ crayons of this colour.

8. ☐ crayons are not yellow.

True or false?

9. There are six more green crayons than purple.

10. There are six fewer red crayons than blue.

The head teacher at a school asked every pupil to choose an activity for sports day. The bar chart below shows the results:

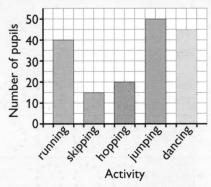

1. What was the most popular activity, and how many pupils chose it?

2. What was the least popular activity, and how many pupils chose it?

3. How many more pupils chose dancing than running?

4. How many fewer pupils chose hopping than running?

5. How many pupils were asked in total?

A pet shop sells four different breeds of rabbits. The bar chart below shows the number of three of the breeds in the shop:

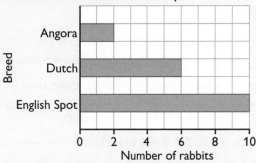

The number of Dwarf Lop rabbits is more than the number of Dutch, but less than the number of English Spot rabbits. There are an even number of Dwarf Lop rabbits.

6. How many Dwarf Lop rabbits are there?

The rabbits are often sold in pairs.

7. How many **pairs** of each breed of rabbit are there?

8. How many more pairs of English Spot rabbits are there than pairs of Angora rabbits?

The bar chart below shows the number of people living in each house on a street:

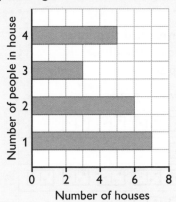

1. How many people live alone?

2. How many people live on the street?

There are thirty houses on the street in total, including empty houses. The empty houses are not shown on the chart.

3. How many houses are empty?

4. How many more houses are not empty than are empty?

Laura is learning French. She learnt 100 new French words over five weeks. She made the bar chart below to show the number of new words she learnt each week:

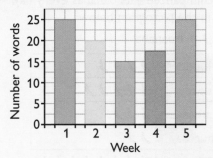

Her mum pointed out that one of the bars must be wrong.

5. Which bar must be wrong? Why?

6. If only one of the bars is wrong, work out the correct height of this bar.

In week 6, Laura learnt two fewer words than she did in her best weeks.

7. How many new words did she learn in week 6?

8. How many more is this than her worst week?

I can solve problems using information in bar charts.

Solving Problems with Pictograms

The key to solving pictogram problems is... the key!

Examples

Four friends have made friendship bracelets.
The pictogram on the right shows how many each friend made:

So (stands for 1 bracelet.

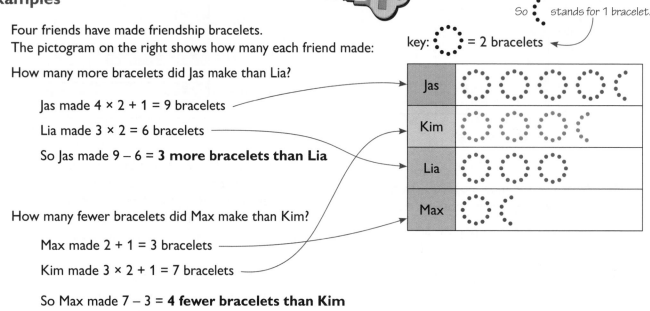

key: ( ) = 2 bracelets

How many more bracelets did Jas make than Lia?

Jas made 4 × 2 + 1 = 9 bracelets

Lia made 3 × 2 = 6 bracelets

So Jas made 9 – 6 = **3 more bracelets than Lia**

How many fewer bracelets did Max make than Kim?

Max made 2 + 1 = 3 bracelets

Kim made 3 × 2 + 1 = 7 bracelets

So Max made 7 – 3 = **4 fewer bracelets than Kim**

Max makes an extra five bracelets. Add this information to Max's row on the pictogram.

Five bracelets = 2 + 2 + 1 = ( ) ( ) (

Add this to the ( ) (already there:

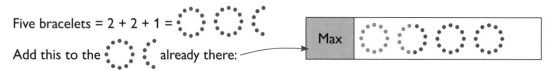

Set A

Chip the chimpanzee eats bananas every day, as shown in the pictogram below:

key: 🍌 = 1 banana

Monday	🍌🍌🍌🍌
Tuesday	🍌🍌🍌🍌🍌
Wednesday	🍌🍌🍌
Thursday	🍌🍌
Friday	🍌🍌🍌🍌🍌🍌🍌🍌

1. How many more bananas did Chip eat on Friday than on Monday?

2. How many fewer bananas did he eat on Wednesday than on Tuesday?

On Saturday Chip ate three more bananas than he did on Thursday. On Sunday Chip ate two fewer bananas than he did on Monday.

3. Copy the pictogram and add rows for Saturday and Sunday.

4. How many bananas did Chip eat in the whole week?

Four dominoes players had a contest.
The pictogram below shows how many games each player won:

key: [•|•] = won 2 games

Ann	[•|•] [•|•] [•|•] [•|•]
Bob	[•|•]
Cath	[•|•] [•|•] [•|•] [•|•] [•|•]
Don	[•|•] [•|•]

5. Fill in the gaps below with the players' names, in order of the number of games they won. The player who won the most games should be in 1st place:

1st [ ], 2nd [ ], 3rd [ ], 4th [ ]

6. How many more games did the player in 1st place win than the player in 4th place?

7. The player in 2nd place won 4 more games than they lost. How many games did they lose?

8. The player in 3rd place lost twice as many games as they won. How many games did they lose?

Some pupils plant seeds in 4 different pots to see which ones grow best. They plant 10 seeds in each pot.

The pictogram below shows how many of the seeds in each pot have sprouted after one day:

key: ⬭ = 2 seeds sprouted

Pot A	⬭ ⬭ ⬭ ⬭
Pot B	⬭ ⬭ ⬬
Pot C	⬬
Pot D	⬭ ⬬

1   How many more seeds sprouted in pot A than pot B?

2   How many fewer seeds sprouted in pot C than pot D?

After two days:
All the seeds had sprouted in pot A.
Three more seeds had sprouted in pot B.
No more seeds had sprouted in pot C.
The number of sprouted seeds in pot D had doubled.

3   Make a new pictogram to show the number of sprouted seeds in each pot after two days.

At a rock show, fans of the band are asked to vote for their favourite band member.
The votes are shown in the pictogram below:

key: ⊠ = 4 votes

Singer	⊠ ⊠ ⊠ ⊠ ⊠
Guitarist	⊠ ⊠ ⊠ ⊠ ⋉
Bass player	⊠ ⊠ ⊠
Drummer	⊠ ⊠ ⊠ ⊠ ⊠ ▲

True or false?

4   The drummer got three more votes than the guitarist.

5   The bass player got five fewer votes than the singer.

6   The bass player got half as many votes as the drummer.

The keyboard player got four more votes than the bass player.

7   Draw an extra row of the pictogram to show this.

In a game of tiddlywinks, four players take turns to flick coloured disks (called 'winks') into a pot. The aim is to get as many winks as possible into the pot.

The pictogram below shows the number of winks in the pot at the end of a game:

Player	key: ● = 2 winks
green	● ◗
red	● ● ●
blue	◖
yellow	● ● ◗

1   How many more winks did the highest scoring player get into the pot than the lowest scoring player?

2   The players are actually on two teams. Red & blue are team 1, and green & yellow are team 2. The team with the most winks in the pot in total wins the game.

How many more winks did the winning team score than the losing team?

A group of friends are playing dice games. They earn points for winning games. They want to record their points in the pictogram below:

key: ⚃ = 5 points

Ada	⚃ ⚃ ⚃ ⚀
Bella	
Carl	
Dylan	
Ed	

Copy and complete the pictogram using the following information:

3   Bella has three more points than Ada.

4   Bella has five more points than Carl.

5   Dylan has the same number of points as Ada and Carl have in total.

6   When the friends are listed in order of their number of points (most to least), Ed is in 4th place.

I can solve problems using information in pictograms.

Statistics — Review 2

The table below shows the number of each type of fish in an aquarium:

Fish	Frequency
Goldfish	9
Sharks	5
Swordfish	?
Clownfish	3

(1) How many more goldfish are there than sharks?

(2) How many fewer clownfish are there than sharks?

There are twice the number of swordfish as there are clownfish.

(3) How many swordfish are there?

(4) How many fish are there in total?

(5) How many fish are not sharks?

The ages of children at a board games club are shown below:

Age:	6	7	8	9	10
Frequency:	3	6	7	2	2

True or false?

(6) There are eight 7-year-olds.

(7) Four children are aged 9 or 10.

(8) There are the same number of 8- and 9-year-olds.

(9) There are nine children under 8.

(10) There are half as many 6-year-olds as 7-year-olds.

The bar chart below shows the number of three different types of tree in a park:

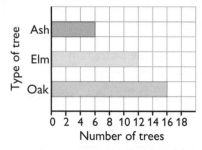

(11) How many more oak trees are there than elm trees?

(12) How many fewer ash trees are there than oak trees?

(13) How many ash and elm trees are there altogether?

The owner of a chip shop asked her customers: "What is the best sauce to dip your chips into?" Their answers are shown on the bar chart below:

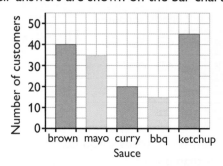

True or false?

(14) 50 customers chose the most popular sauce.

(15) 15 customers chose the least popular sauce.

(16) 10 more customers chose ketchup than mayo.

(17) Brown sauce was twice as popular as curry sauce.

(18) The chip shop owner asked exactly 100 people.

The pictogram below shows the number of days when it snowed in one town in three different months.

key: ❄ = 2 snowy days

December	❄ ❄
January	❄ ❄ ❄ ❄
February	❄ ❄ ❄

(19) How many more snowy days were there in January than December?

(20) How many fewer snowy days were there in February than January?

(21) How many snowy days were there in total in December, January and February?

(22) Ralph makes a pictogram to show how many dogs he saw on his daily walk on Monday:

key: ◷ = 3 dogs | Mon | ◷ ◷ ◷ ◖ |

On Tuesday he saw two more dogs than on Monday, and four more dogs than on Wednesday. On Thursday he saw twice as many dogs as on Wednesday. On Friday he saw three fewer dogs than he did on Thursday.

Copy and complete the pictogram for Friday:

Fri	

You really tackled those tricky tasks — well done!

1 For her maths homework, Nancy asked people in her family what their favourite fruit is.
She recorded their answers in a tally chart, but Nancy's naughty rabbit Nibbles ate parts of the page!

She can remember the following facts:

*   The most popular fruit was oranges.

*   She asked twelve people in total.

*   Three people said that bananas were their favourite.

*   Peaches were twice as popular as grapes.

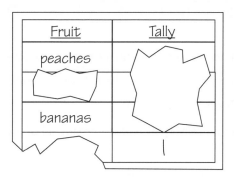

Naughty Nibbles

a)   Copy Nancy's tally chart and fill in the missing information. Add and fill in a frequency column too.

b)   Design your own table to record information about people's favourite fruits.

2 Ben asks ten people how they got to school that day.
He shows the information on the bar chart on the right.

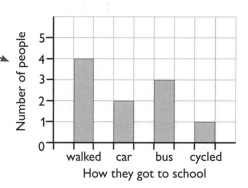

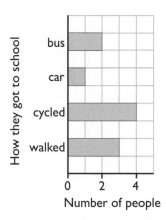

Jen asks ten **other** people the same question.
She shows the information on the bar chart on the left.

a)   Copy the table on the right.
Combine Ben and Jen's results to complete the table. ——————→

b)   Copy the bar chart below. Use the table to complete
the bar chart showing the combined information.

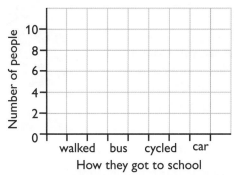

How they got to school	Number of people
walked	
bus	
cycled	
car	

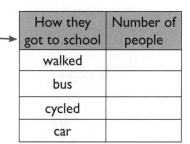

c)   Ask ten people in your class how they got to school today.
Record the answers in a table.
Draw a bar chart to show this information.

3   Marty is having a party. He wants to know what his twenty guests would like to eat.

On the invitations he asks two questions, and records the answers in two tables:

Do you like jelly?

Answer:	Yes	No	Don't know
Frequency:	8	10	2

Do you like ice-cream?

Answer:	Yes	No	Don't know
Frequency:	12	7	1

Marty thinks: 8 people like jelly and 12 people like ice-cream.

8 + 12 = 20 people like jelly or ice-cream.

There are 20 guests.

So if I serve jelly and ice-cream, all of my guests will be happy.

Explain why Marty might be wrong.

4   Forgetful Flo finds this bar chart in her notebook:

She has forgotten what it shows!

a)   Write a list of five things the bar chart could be showing.

b)   Swap lists with another person. Pick your favourite idea from their list. Write five different facts from the bar chart, using the idea you have chosen.

For example: if the chart showed the numbers of coloured sweets in a jar, one fact would be that there are 50 yellow sweets...

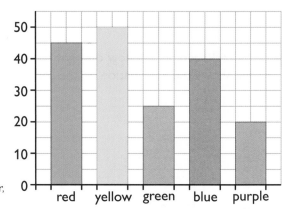

5

Pirate	Gold coins found
Greeneye	◯ ◯
Rusty	◯ ◯ ◯
Purplebeard	◯ ◯ ◯ ◯
Scarlet	◯ ◯ ◯

A band of pirates have been on a treasure hunt.

They each found a different number of gold coins, and kept a record of their coins in the pictogram on the left.

But one important piece of information is missing...

...the pirates didn't make a key!

Purplebeard

I be the best pirate, arr... I found twice as many coins as Captain Greeneye!

Avast ye! I found five more coins than Captain Greeneye!

Rusty

Use what they say above to make a key for the pirates' pictogram.

Then use the key to work out how many gold coins the four pirates found in total.

Glossary and Index

2D shape	A <u>flat shape</u>, e.g. a square or a triangle. p118-119, p122
3D shape	A <u>solid shape</u>, e.g. a cube or a sphere. p120-121, p123-124
acute angle	An angle that measures <u>less than 90°</u>. It is <u>smaller</u> than a <u>right angle</u>. p114
add, +	<u>Put together</u> two numbers to find the <u>total</u>. For example, '12 + 7 = 19' is '12 add 7 = 19'. p22-25, p32-34, p42-45, p80
analogue	An analogue clock has <u>hands</u> to show the hours, minutes and seconds. p102-103
angle	A measure of how far something has <u>turned</u>. p113-114
bar chart	A method of recording data. The height of a bar shows the amount of a quantity. p131-132, p138-139
capacity	The amount something can hold when it's <u>full</u>. Capacity is usually measured in <u>litres</u> or <u>millilitres</u>. p94-95
centimetre, cm	A unit for measuring <u>length</u> or <u>distance</u>. There are 100 cm in a metre. p90-91
change (money)	The money left over when you buy something. p100
circle	A perfectly round, <u>flat shape</u>. p118
cone	A solid shape. It has a circular base and a curved surface that comes to a point. p120-121
cube	A solid '<u>box</u>' shape with six <u>square faces</u>. p120-121, p123-124
cuboid	A solid '<u>box</u>' shape with six <u>rectangular faces</u>. p120-121, p123-124
cylinder	A solid '<u>tube</u>' shape. It has two identical circular faces and one curved surface. p120-121
day	A unit of <u>time</u>. There are 24 hours in a day, and 7 days in a week. p105
decimal point	The <u>dot</u> you write in a <u>decimal number</u>. It comes between <u>pounds</u> and <u>pence</u> when writing amounts of money. p99-100
denominator	The bottom number of a <u>fraction</u>. p71-85
digit	A digit is one of these numbers: 0, 1, 2, 3, 4, 5, 6, 7, 8 or 9. p2-4
digital	A digital clock shows the time as numbers, for example, 08:30. p104
divide, ÷	<u>Share</u> equally or put into equal <u>groups</u>. For example, 6 ÷ 3 means 6 divided by 3, or 6 shared into 3 equal groups. (The answer is 2.) p53, p56-58, p62-66
edge	Where two <u>faces</u> join on a <u>3D shape</u>. p120-121

Glossary and Index

equivalent fractions	Fractions which are <u>written differently</u> but are <u>equal to</u> each other. For example, $\frac{3}{6}$ and $\frac{1}{2}$. p75-76
estimate	An estimate is a <u>sensible guess</u> at the answer. You can use <u>rounding</u> to help you estimate answers. p40
face	A <u>flat shape</u> that makes up a 3D shape. p120-121
fraction	Part of a whole number or shape. p71-85
frequency	How many times something happens. p129-130, p136-137
gram, g	A unit for measuring <u>mass</u>. 1 kilogram = 1000 grams. p92-93
hemisphere	A solid shape. It's <u>half</u> of a <u>sphere</u>. p121
heptagon	A flat shape with <u>seven straight sides</u>. p118-119, p122
hexagon	A flat shape with <u>six straight sides</u>. p118-119, p122
horizontal	Going <u>across</u>. Shelves and table tops are horizontal. p115-116
hour	A unit of <u>time</u>. An hour is 60 minutes. There are 24 hours in a day. p102-104, p106-108
inverse	<u>Opposite</u>. For example, addition and subtraction are <u>inverse operations</u>. p41
kilogram, kg	A unit for measuring <u>mass</u>. 1 kilogram = 1000 grams. p92-93
length	A measure of <u>how long</u> or <u>how far</u> something is. Millimetres, centimetres and metres are all units of length. p90-91
litre, l	A unit for measuring <u>volume</u> or <u>capacity</u>. 1 litre = 1000 millilitres. Orange juice often comes in 1 litre cartons. p94-95
mass	A measure of <u>how heavy</u> something is. Mass is usually measured in kilograms or grams. p92-93
metre, m	A unit for measuring <u>length</u> or <u>distance</u>. 1 metre = 100 centimetres. A door is about 2 m high. p90-91
millilitre, ml	A unit for measuring <u>volume</u> or <u>capacity</u>. There are 1000 millilitres in a litre. A teaspoon has a capacity of about 5 ml. p94-95
millimetre, mm	A unit for measuring <u>length</u> or <u>distance</u>. 1000 millimetres = 1 metre, and 10 millimetres = 1 centimetre. p90-91

Glossary and Index

minute	A unit of <u>time</u>. There are 60 minutes in an hour, and 60 seconds in a minute. p102-104, p106-108
money	Used to pay for things. In the UK, it is measured in <u>pounds</u> and <u>pence</u>. p99-100
month	A unit of <u>time</u>. There are 12 months in a year (January to December). p105
multiple	Multiples are the numbers in a <u>times table</u>. For example, the multiples of 4 are 4, 8, 12, 16... p9-12, p50-52
multiply, ×	The proper maths word for 'times'. p50-52, p55, p58, p60-61, p63-66
numerator	The top number of a fraction. p71-85
obtuse angle	An angle that measures <u>more than</u> 90° but less than 180°. It is <u>between</u> one and two <u>right angles</u>. p114
octagon	A flat shape with <u>eight straight sides</u>. p118-119, p122
octahedron	A 3D shape with <u>8 faces</u>. p121, p124
ordering	Putting <u>in order</u>. For example, to order 3, 1 and 2 from smallest to largest, start with the smallest, then the next smallest: 1, 2, 3. p6, p77-78, p90, p92, p94
parallel lines	Lines that point in exactly the same direction and are always the <u>same distance apart</u>. p115-116
partition	<u>Split</u> a number up. You can partition numbers in many ways. For example, 173 = 100 + 70 + 3 or 173 = 150 + 20 + 3. p5, p25, p30
pentagon	A flat shape with <u>five straight sides</u>. p118-119, p122
perimeter	The <u>distance</u> around the outside of a 2D shape. p97-98
perpendicular lines	Lines that meet each other at <u>right angles</u> (or would meet at right angles if you extended them) are perpendicular. p115-116
pictogram	A method of recording data. Pictures represent an amount of something, and this amount is shown in a key next to the pictogram. p133-134, p140-141
place value	A digit's value in a number depends on its <u>position</u> in the number. Each position has a different <u>place value</u>. For example, the value of 2 in 827 is 2 tens. p2
prism	A solid shape with <u>two identical faces</u> at either end. p120-121, p123-124
pyramid	A <u>solid shape</u>. Its base can be any straight-sided shape. The other <u>faces</u> all meet at a point. p120-121, p123-124

Glossary and Index

quadrilateral	A flat shape with <u>four straight sides</u>. p118-119, p122	
rectangle	A <u>quadrilateral</u> with <u>two pairs of equal sides</u> and <u>four right angles</u>. p118-119, p122	
right angle	A <u>quarter turn</u>, or 90°. p113-116	
scale	The numbered marks on a line that help you measure things. p90, p92, p94	
second	A unit of <u>time</u>. There are 60 seconds in a minute. p106	
sphere	A round '<u>ball</u>' shape. p120-121	
square	A <u>quadrilateral</u> with <u>four equal sides</u> and <u>four right angles</u>. p118-119, p122	
subtract, −	Take away one number from another. For example, '11 − 6 = 5' is '11 take away 6 = 5' or '11 subtract 6 = 5'. p27-30, p36-38, p42-45, p81	
table	A method of organising and recording data into rows and columns. p129-130, p136-137	
tenth	You get a tenth of something when you split it into <u>ten equal parts</u>, or <u>divide it by ten</u>. One tenth is written as $\frac{1}{10}$. p72-73	
tetrahedron	A 3D shape with <u>4 faces</u>. p120-121	
triangle	A flat shape with <u>three straight sides</u>. p118-119, p122	
vertex	A corner on a 3D shape, where at least <u>three faces</u> or <u>edges</u> meet. <u>Vertices</u> is the word for more than one vertex. p120-121	
vertical	Going straight <u>up and down</u>. Walls and flag poles are vertical. p115-116	
year	A unit of <u>time</u>. There are 12 months in a year, or 365 days. A leap year has 366 days. p105	

M3PB21